Afrikan Woman the Original Guardian Angel

A collection of writings on the Black Woman's creation of and on-going contribution to world civilization

Ishakamusa Barashango

AFRIKAN WORLD BOOKS
2217 Pennsylvania Ave., Baltimore, MD 21217
410-383-2006
www.afrikanworldbooks.com

October 2001

NEW EDITION

First Printing **December, 1989**

Cover: Mr. Cal Massey

DEDICATION

This book is dedicated to a Trinity of some of the many Black Women who have been so essential in my life.

To "Sister": my genetic mother, who through the pangs of birth bore me to this world down the Divine Canal of the fallopian tube through the Heavenly gates of the vulva major past the Sacred monuments of her jet black thighs and into the warmth and comfort of her Holy bosom. Though she joined the realm of our Ancestors in the spirit world a year after my delivery, the beauty and strength of this Afrikan angel will always be a source of comfort and inspiration to my soul through all eternity.

To Miss Lottie: who cared for all of the children on the street where we lived while many of our parents did "day's work" in the suburbs. No one seems to have known her last name. We just called her "Miss Lottie". I can see visions of her now, even as I write, sitting in her living room window; this strong, full-sized Black Woman who to all of us children was the epitome of care and loving discipline.

To the Reverend Mother Susie Tate: my spiritual mother and clairvoyant who through deep spiritual insight and her special connection with the Creator has over the years helped to guide me through many a difficult period; even unto saving my mortal life on several occasions.

ART CREDITS

Cover Art:	Essence Art Reproductions 929-8 Lincoln Avenue Holbrook, NY 11741
Ausar Trinity	Brother Metu Teggkhet Ausar-Auset Society Brooklyn, NY

Dr. Ishakamusa Barashango
April 27, 1938 - January 14, 2004

AFRIKAN WORLD BOOKS
2217 Pennsylvania Ave., Baltimore, MD 21217
410-383-2006
www.afrikanworldbooks.com

FOREWORD

Afrikan Woman: The Original Guardian Angel is a collection of scholarly essays* on the origin of the historical concept of angels and its relationship to the role of the Black Woman in the creation of and on-going contribution to the arts and sciences of world civilization.

The first essay is taken from a seminar on Angelology conducted by Dr. Barashango at the Malcolm X Building of the House of Umoja Project in Garvey Square at Richard Allen City (Philadelphia, Pennsylvania).

The second offering is taken from the same seminar and reflects on the significance of angel psycho-pictography such as seraphims and firebirds in the ancient High Culture civilization of Kemet (Egypt). The profound meaning of the power of the sapphire throne of ancient Afrikan rulers is also defined and discussed.

The third essay, also drawn from the Angelology studies, deals with the subject of cherubims as scientific symbolic representations of protective forces in nature. Griffins, gargoyles and other angel-related images are also examined in this essay.

The following three essays, Sapphire Eve: Divine Mother of the Universal Egg, Rhapsody to the Glorious Queen of Heaven and Black Woman: The Primogineal Bird of Paradise, are excerpted from the manuscript of the forthcoming work, *Afrikan Genesis: An Historical Reality*, by this author. Each of these in their turn provide us with some historical information as to how the original Black Woman came to be regarded all over the world in such an ethereal and revered manner.

Essay Seven is a composite of comments and ideas delivered at the Sojourner Truth Adolescent Rites of Passage Conference, convened at Howard University February 18, 1989, and focuses on the integral function of Afrikan Women as the original guardian angels in the last rite of passage.

The final offering is in actuality a descriptive preview of the soon to be published work *Afrikan Genesis: An Historical Reality* which consistently re-emphasizes the role of Afrikan Women in human enlightenment and world civilization.

We trust that our readers will find each of these pieces to be both informative and edifying in their personal quest for greater knowledge and understanding of the true realities of our glorious Afrikan heritage.

The Publishers

* We dub these scholarly essays because they are documenting writings which transcend the opinion of the author and are somewhat lengthier than the average format of this type.

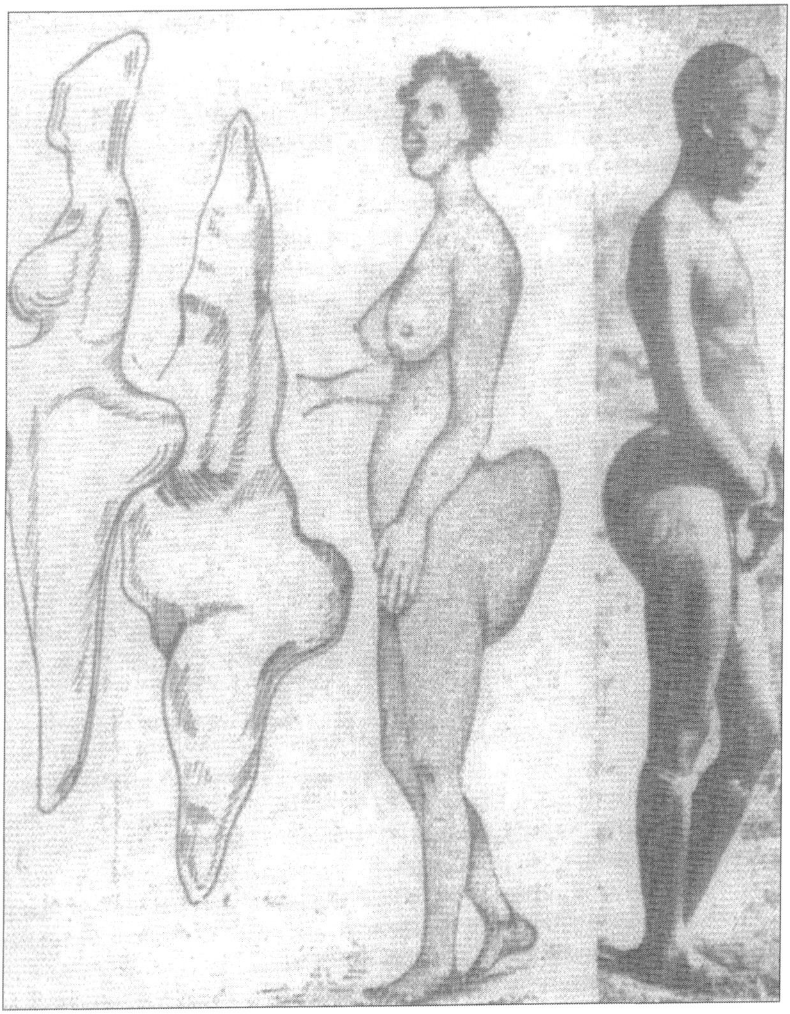

IV. Left to right: Two Grimaldi carvings of about 15,000 B. C., showing the steatopygy, or development of fat on the buttocks. Venus Kallipygos, or the celebrated Hottentot Venus of the last century, from a model of her in the Museum d'Ethnologie, Paris. (Winchell). A living Hottentot woman of the Kalahari, South Africa. (See also No. 5, Sex and Race, Vol. I.)

TABLE OF CONTENTS

INTRODUCTION

BLACK WOMAN: THE EPITOME OF BEAUTY AND WISDOM IN THE ANCIENT WORLD

It is our hope and prayer that reiteration of the historical data presented in this work will contribute to the realization that the standards and trends of physical beauty as manifested in feminine physique, hair styles, cosmetics and fashions were first set by the original Black Woman. For she collectively held the position of Ms. Universe for untold successive generations. Yes, overwhelming archaeological, anthropological and historical documentation has revealed beyond a shadow of a doubt that the Afrikan Woman was the first beauty queen on Earth and the adoration of her exquisite comeliness so inspired the imagination of human creative thought that she was projected into the heavens.

At that time in history, between 100,000-18,000 years ago, it appears that all Black Women in the world felt very good about themselves because there was not even an inkling of a doubt as to her being the sheer essence of feminine pulchritude. For long extended periods of human history, the whole world revered and literally worshipped the Afrikan Woman. In fact, the first sacredotal objects of veneration were replicas of the female anatomy. In terms of historical reality, all religious symbols, i.e. the cross, the star and the crescent, the star of David, etc., can be traced back to the Black Woman's body because she was once regarded by the ancients as the supreme divine vessel of life. This particular subject is rather thoroughly explored and discussed in the aforementioned work *Afrikan Genesis: An Historical Reality*.

Dr. Yusef ben Jochannon, as do all truly enlightened Afro-centric scholars, says that in his opinion, the Afrikan Woman is still the real standard of beauty in the world today. Therefore, my beloved Sisters, as the scriptures declare, "Rejoice greatly, O daughter of Zion." Take off the sack cloth of blues and hurt songs and adorn yourselves with your original Afrikan glory. Let the Black Woman come to understand that she does not need to continue attacking her face and hair in the futile effort of trying to look like somebody else. Sister, you are the one. To the real Black Man, you are the y true woman. Scientifically speaking, for hundreds of thousands-maybe millions of years, before there was any other kind of woman on planet Earth, there was you and yours was the most valued and desired beauty in the universe.

One of the main themes that keeps emerging during our research and studies in the various disciplines of Afrikanology is the irrefutable fact that without the joys of the feminine gender the world would self-destruct. Of course, most men can appreciate this on a physical level, but it is the spiritual energy generated by this sexual unity that makes union with a woman so potent. This Om-Um, Ying-Yang activating principle is reflected in everything throughout the universe from the minutest atom to the remotest galaxy.

As evidenced, Puritanical societies where sexual harmony is repressed tend to be more violent and aggressive. Now I am not citing this in a spirit of abject promiscuity or to emphasis mere biological gratification, but rather as a re-affirmation of ancient Afrikan High Culture societies' general attitudes toward and genuine concern for the achievement of a cosmic balance in human sexuality. This is one of the hallmarks of these original civilizations before the disruption of foreign invaders who were generally discontent with themselves and their native habitations as well as suffering from myriad pathologies such as "ambiguous sexual dimorphism" and "phycho-sexual maladjustment".

The role of the Black Woman in the establishment of civilization is irrefutable for she made possible all the treasures of civilization we now hold so dear. From time immemorial, man has depended upon woman for the development of the arts and sciences of civilization. This is especially true of the original Afrikan Race, the first people on Earth. So profound was the Afrikan Woman's contribution to the growth and advancement of humanity that she was enshrined in the hearts of the people of the early civilizations as the Queen of Heaven, the Mother Goddess, the Creatress of All Living Things and her earthly daughters were adored by Black Men as angels of light of whom it was said that no man could achieve total knowledge of God without complete oneness with her. She was the first true civilizing force on Earth. It is because of her that we are able to eat an abundant variety of healthy and tasteful foods, live in houses, write the alphabet, record time, reckon mathematics and conduct ourselves in the world with some semblance of civility.

The superb actor and scholar, Avery Brooks of *A Man Called Hawk* fame, reminds us that the ancient scriptures say "that woman is wisdom and wisdom is the breath of God". Unfortunately, some brothers may be a little less than comfortable with the resurgence of this knowledge Nevertheless, I suggest an awakening to the historical reality—that all available scientific evidence reveals—that it was the Black Woman who first came to the understanding of and implemented the principles of civilization should not in any way cause the Black Man to feel the need to indulge the machoism of male chauvinistic insecurities. For if the truth be known, from the very beginning of human history to the present, the Creator intended the Afrikan Male and Female to run the world as equal partners in power and glory.

Herein lies the secret of our true strength as men; our acceptance of the divinity of the Afrikan Woman and the complete internalization of the lifestyles and values inherent in that reality. Then and only then will the rest of the world respect us as real men. I invite you, my brothers, to mentally and spiritually get into the deep mystery of this concept and experience what it can do for the expansion of your consciousness.

At this point I would quote the words of an apparently strong and secure young Black Man who also loves Black Women with all his heart and soul, Brother Walter Beasley, as he reminds the Black Male and Female, "Those outside of us benefit the most from our discord."

Therefore, one of the intents and purposes of the publishers is that this offering will help to foster a stronger bond, a more profound understanding and a greater appreciation of the Black Man and Woman for each other. For there is no greater love on Earth that theirs when it is sincerely and naturally expressed.

1

AN AFRO-CENTRIC PERSPECTIVE ON THE ORIGIN OF ANGELS

According to Albert Churchward, the first concept of angels evolved out of the human-headed bird symbols of Kemetan (ancient Egyptian) iconography.[1] See Plate 1. Barbara Walker informs us that "Because birds traveled freely between the earthly and heavenly realms, they were everywhere regarded as angelic messengers, givers of omens, possessors of occult secrets, as well as soul-carriers. Carrion crows and vultures took souls to heaven. Storks brought them back to Earth for rebirth. Wise owls told the secrets of the night; lustful doves and nightingales told the secrets of love. Angelic eagles foretold the future."[2]

In antiquity angels were regarded as "Dispensors of Joy" and bestowers of light and understanding. Wise priestly professors of ancient Afrikan astro-mythological scientific symbology taught that each person had a guardian angel which was also called a genius or genie. This spiritual entity which represented the essence of human genius was generally described as the feminine anima of inspiration a learned reference to the fact that man first acquired scientific knowledge through the creative genius of Afrikan Women.*Funk and Wagnall's Standard Desk Dictionary*, Volume I, definition #4, says that "In ancient mythology" the word genius denoted "a supernatural being appointed to guide a person throughout life". The French word genius as used in the English language comes from the Latin *gignere* meaning variously "to beget, bear, produce or give life" and the Greek *genesthai*-"to be born". It is also related to the word "genie" from the Arabic *jinn*. In literary translations, it generally refers to a person with exceptional powers; often considered to be magical. In short, the term genius loosely translated signifies an inspirational force that engenders the higher intellect, a posture originally accorded the feminine energies in the cosmos.

The role of Afrikan Women in the cerebral sphere is clearly set forth in the Hebrew rendering of the phrase "Holy Ghost", Ruach

Qodesh meaning a vital stimulating force especially one that influences the mind. In Kushite-India, it was known as the *kundalini* "the serpentine fire of wisdom and universal enlightenment" to the High Culture scientists of old Hindu-Kush, this principle was also known as the *shakti*, a man's eternal soulmate manifested on the earthly plane through the woman or women in his life and as the cosmic spirit which "took him into her ecstatic embrace at death".[3] This concept is still portrayed in modern art when martyrs and fallen heroes are depicted in statuary and other media as being borne to heaven by giant angels.

As an extension of the imagery of the winged goddesses of ancient Kush (Ethiopia) and Kemet (Egypt), one of the earliest forms of angel art takes us back to the empire of Sumer. The Black Men and Women of Sumer created a fabulous empire with outstanding astronomers, a system of cuneiform script and a very high degree of civilization.[4] One of their kings Ur Nammu (c. 2100 BCE) is shown engraved on a stele with a protecting angel hovering above his head as he reverently bows in prayer. The angel in holding pattern over this ancient Black rulers head is the symbol of something and we will find out as we continue our investigation what that symbol is.

Journalist Edgar J. Ridley reminds us that one of the main contributing factors to the problems which plague Black People today is the general unwillingness or inability to distinguish symbol from reality. All too often, we take the symbol to be real and when a person believes that the symbol of something is in fact the thing it represents, they become totally confused.[5] Therefore, one of the priorities of Afro-centric scholars is to help separate the symbol from actuality and clarify the fact that what one sees in images and artwork is a symbol of something else, something that is in fact real.

THE TRANSMOGRIFICATION OF ANGELS IN HEBREW-ISRAELITE LITERATURE

The ageless Afrikan concept of winged protectors stylized in the visual arts of Kemet, Sumer, Babylonia, Persia and many other original Kushite nations was eventually incorporated into the philosophy, literature and graphic arts of another, through rather small, Kushite nation known as Hebrews. Poetic visions in the book of Daniel illustrate the Israelite assimilation of Kemetan and Sumerian angelology in the following pictographic manner.

> "I beheld till the thrones were cast down, and the Ancient of days did sit, whose garment was white as snow, and the hair of his head like the pure wool: his throne was like the fiery flame, and his wheels as burning fire. A fiery stream issued and came forth before him: thousand thousands ministered unto him, and ten thousand times ten thousands stood before him: the judgement was set, and the books were opened."[6]

The LIVING BIBLE renders "thousands upon thousands ministered unto him" thusly "Millions of angels ministered to him . . . ". For further explanation of this text and its relevance to the Afrikoid images of the Supreme Being in early religious writings and iconography, see *God, the Bible, and the Black Man's Destiny*, Chapters 1 and 2 by this author. As pertaining to our present pursuit, we will encounter this judgement scene again in its original Afrikan setting in Essay 2. At this point, however, we would remind you that the concept of angels did not originate in the Bible. During the period of Earth's history when these ideas began to circulate, about 100,000 years ago, there were no Hebrews anywhere in the world. Because as a distinct nation-state, the Israelites did not appear until well after 1200 BCE and only began to compile a literature somewhere between the 8th and 5th Centuries before the common era.

Though most of us were first introduced to the notion of angels via Judeo-Christian teachings, we must come to understand the historical reality that this idea came to us through the influence of the church rather than as a product of its own creation.

The word angel as used in the English language is from the Greek *aggelos* meaning "messenger". The same being so in the Hebrew *mal'ak* and the Arabic *malik*. Initially the designation referred to a messenger, one who was on a mission with a message and usually denoted a human rather than a superhuman being. In terms of a strict scientific definition, this is how the word angel was applied. However, in the High Culture Science of many ancient Afrikan civilizations, the angel symbol had an esoteric as well as a practical function.

The perception of angels in ancient Hebrew theology was directly related to the evolution of anthropomorphism (that is to say the attribution of human qualities to the Supreme Deity) in their cultural worldview. This brings us to how, why and when the concept developed among them. Albert E. Bailey, in the book *Daily Life in Bible Times* informs us that after the Babylonians, in 587 BCE, utterly demolished Jerusalem, the capitol of Judea, and led the Hebrews off into captivity, the sacerdotal class of the bonded population responded to the dilemma thusly.

". . . because of their deportation the priests were out of a job, and both they and the prophets had to find some new channel of religious activity. They therefore took up teaching. They turned towards the past, to the stories of their national heroes and the incidents of their tumultuous history; they set themselves to interpret it all in the light of religion and to rewrite it as a series of lessons for the admonition and guidance of future generations. Thus they changed what had been story and history into a textbook of religious education, sagas and chronicles into a Bible."[7]

Here Bailey gets right to the point by simply stating that the priests and prophets "were out of a job", yet they were creative and innovative enough to develop something which would provide them with employment. Thus the whole thing about angels and other elements of Hebrew theological mythology was born out of the clergy's need to find a way of making a living. They were desperate to come up with a mechanism for getting the people's attention again. Now that they were in Babylon, the herd mentality of the masses was no longer at their disposal because the devout suppliant did not have to come up to the temple and pay money for the cows, the bulls, the turtles and everything else the priests had to cut open for the sacrifice and sprinkle blood on. In fact the general attitude of the Israelite people towards the ecclesiastical aristocracy was "we don't need you anymore, what can you do for us, why you don't even have a temple." So the sacerdotal class in the process of solving these problems evolved a whole body of literature based on and oft times drawn directly from the Kushite, Kemetan, Sumerian, Babylonian, Persian, Indian and other ancient Afrikan High Culture principles and precepts in circulation at the time.

In their formulation of *sacred scriptures*, the Israelite priests and scribes inculcated the idea of an angel being more than just a human messenger. This continued to mushroom into an increasing emphasis on divine transcendence which resulted in the reluctance to ascribe to Yahweh certain activities. Thus in later Hebrew theology the Lord God no longer reveals himself directly but through an angel to his prophets. So the concept of there being supernatural flying angels soaring through the air for sundry reasons became an ever recurring theme in Hebrew literature. Israelite priests had also observed that Kemetan and Babylonian kings and dignitaries often had what was called interpreters. Not that anyone had to interpret for them but protocol dedicated that no one except the royal family and certain members of the nobility could talk directly to the king. So the Hebrew clergy figured if men do this on Earth naturally their supreme deity should do likewise in heaven. Thus they created for him in their literature supernatural messengers in the form of angels. Unfortunately, because of their male chauvinistic point of view, they transmogrified the original Afrikan Female angelic scientific symbols into neuter-males.

Here it may be fitting to mention that the Babylonian Empire was an offshoot of the ancient Sumerians. Dr. John G. Jackson tells us that the Babylonians found Sumer's High Culture civilization in tact and never advanced it beyond the point from which they inherited it when they came into the land and by military force took it over.[8]

From the time of their exile in Babylon, angels played a prominent role in Hebrew religious writings. So the stories you read in the Old Testament about Adam and Eve in the Garden of Eden, Abraham, Jacob, Samsom and other folks' encounters with angels are incidents which were supposed to have occurred before the Israelites were taken into captivity in Babylon, but actually these stories were written after the fact. And the reason why a host of angelic beings are depicted administering to the Ancient of days in Daniel's vision is because the book of Daniel itself was not written until around 200 BCE.

Enclclopedia Britannica says that angel was " . . . a term used in the vocabulary of monotheistic religions to describe a personal being intermediate in nature, status, and powers, between God and man. It may be conjectured that in most instances a belief in such beings is an attempt to retain the subordinate gods and spirits of a polytheistic or an animistic faith which preceded the development of monotheism . . . .Islam and Christianity accepted current Jewish ideas of angels, . . . the religion of the Old Testament recognized many such inferior superhuman beings. Whilst it was strictly monolatrous, and recognized Yahweh alone as an object of worship for Israel, it conceived of Him as dwelling in royal state, surrounded by attendants and servants . . ."[9]

What the reference is conveying here is that this was one way to continue believing in many gods without calling them that. That is why the idea of angels became so prevalent among the Hebrews. Now the ancient Afrikan, from whom the Hebrews who were Afrikans themselves inherited their knowledge, did not feel the need to indulge in such devious tactics because they understood that the different gods and goddesses were merely manifestations of the one God, but in the later developments of Judaism, Islam and Christianity, theologians endeavored to conceal this ancient High Culture concept under the guise of angels and administering spirits. The Bible provides us with a very good example of this in I Kings 22:19. "And he said, here thou therefore the word of the Lord: I saw the Lord sitting on his throne, and all the hosts of heaven standing by him on his right hand and on his left." The idea of the Creator being surrounded by all of these administering spirits and angels was one of the ways the Hebrews used to reconcile the fact that they were never, as they claim today, totally monotheistic.

THE CORRUPTION OF ANGELS IN EURO-CHRISTIAN THEOLOGY

We will soon return to the original concept of angels in the ancient world in the next Essay; however, at this juncture we will lend some attention as to how the ancient Afrikan High Culture Astro-Mythological scientific symbology of angels was co-opted and corrupted in the Euro-Christian tradition. In a word, how and why most people think of angels in the manner in which they do today.

As we have previously stated, originally the term angel literally meant a messenger; a person carrying a message; usually from some great dignitary to someone else and that it was also a symbol of the spiritual power of the feminine energy which motivated and stimulated human intellect. But in European Christian iconography angels became white winged, white robed, long blond haired, blue eyed, harp playing effeminate looking males.

In the early days various opinions were held by Christian theologians as to the nature of angels. Some of the early church fathers spoke of guardian angels and bad angels. Belief in the guardianship of angels and in their participation in the government of the world led to the practice of invoking and venerating them. At first most Christian teachers disapproved of the worship of angels. But at the second Council of Nicea, convened in 787 CE, it was conceded that "though angels were not to receive divine worship they might receive reverential treatment." But until that time, Christians were bowing down to and worshipping angels in much the same manner as they were bowing down to Jesus, God and Mary. In fact, they were bowing down to just about everything. Today devotees of some Christian denominations are still bowing down to divers statues and relics while at the same time disclaiming idolatry. The mention of this is not intended as a value judgement, but rather as an observation because it is ironic that these same people will send missionaries around the world to convert what they call "the heathen" from the idolatry and worship of many gods. Yet, historically speaking, Euro-Christians have been known to maim, murder, displace and enslave whole tribes and nations of people and to wantonly deprive same of the natural resources of their own lands, even unto the outright takeover of countries. All in the name of converting "the heathen" to the religion of the one true God. And yes, some Muslim groups have been guilty of the same atrocities in the name of religion. In this regard, any intelligent person would have to ask the question, who then is the true heathen.

During the Dark Ages in Europe (538-1798 CE) when all scientific investigation was prohibitory, the general populous was not allowed to read the Bible. Only the ecclesiastical aristocracy and very few of them throughout the whole of Europe were literate. At this time the highest form of scientific investigation permitted by law was to determine how many angels you could fit on the head of a stick pin. This was considered to be very serious study in those days. During this same period, the Dogon in west Alkebulan (Afrika) were searching the sky with telescopes. The inhabitants of the old Ghanaian, Mali and Songhai Empires were building houses illuminated by candlelight in the windows while the populations of most European nations were still living in crude windowless hovels with only a chimney chute to let the smoke from hearth fires escape.[10] At the University of Sankore in Timbuktu and other institutions of higher learning, Afrikan physicians were performing cataract and brain surgery among other "high tech" functions. Other thinkers were improving chess board moves originally developed in ancient Kemet (Egypt). From their bases of operation in northern Alkebulan, the Blackamoors took this High Culture which far exceeded anything possessed by European scholars at the time and introduced it to that benighted continent. The enlightened civilization brought to Europe by the Moors became the model for all its later institutions.

Think on this. While you, in the person of your Afrikan Ancestors, were in the process of advancing the evolution of civilization, Europe's learned men were still trying to figure out how many angels you could sit on the head of a stickpin. That's how far this thing on angels went in Euro-Christian culture.

WHAT ARE GUARDIAN ANGELS

As we continue to lay the foundation for understanding the significance of angel symbology in the ancient world before it was co-opted and corrupted by European Christianity, let us examine the true meaning of the concept of guardian angels. In Isaiah 40:21,31 we read,

> "Hast thou not known? hast thou not heard, that the everlasting God, the Lord, the Creator of the ends of the earth, fainteth not, neither is weary there is no searching of his understanding. . . . But they that wait upon the Lord shall renew their strength; they shall mount up with wings as eagles; they shall run, and not be weary and they shall walk, and not faint."

The above text gives us a key as to what angels really meant in the ancient science, mythology and symbolism of Afrikan People. The term wait as employed in the phrase "they that wait upon the Lord" comes from the Hebrew *gavah* meaning "to look and hope for, to expect". It does not imply a standing still or passive stagnation. Without a correct understanding of the language used in ancient High Culture scientific terminology, this particular passage of scripture and others conveying this same thought can and have been much misunderstood, misinterpreted and mistranslated. From what we have been able to ascertain thus far from the rediscovery and study of the intricacies of the philosophical worldview of the ancients, the major objectives of scripture of this genre was to teach the principles of self-motivation and transcendence and it should be remembered that the mainstay of motivation and transcendence in the ancient world was the Afrikan Woman. A fact which will become clearer and clearer as we advance through the succeeding essays.

Another intent of the above text was to demonstrate that even though the Kushite-Hebrews had a fervent belief in the Creator's protective power, it was clearly understood that it was necessary for a person to consciously put themselves in a state of mental being wherein they could attract and receive such protection. "Mounting up like eagles" signified that one must be responsible for the quality of his or her own life. A principle of self-realization that is succinctly stated another way in the old adage "God helps those who help themselves". In other words, belief in divine intervention should not cause you to walk around thinking "I am protected by the Lord so it makes no difference what I do; If I should walk out in the street in front of a moving vehicle, I will be alright for an angel will fly out of the sky and save me in the nick of time". Of course such an action would be ridiculous, not to mention perhaps fatal. Obviously angels were not to serve that purpose, but rather they were in reality symbols that re-emphasized awareness of the motivating inspirational force which emanates from the feminine entity and exhilarates you with the will and enthusiasm to do for self.

Directly related to this idea was the genius provided by the angelic essence of the Afrikan Woman, which during the establishment of the first civilizations gave the people a sense they could achieve whatever they could conceive. That is why the great pyramids and many other megalithic structures originally built by the Black Race all over the planet Earth are still standing today as awesome testimonies to this historical reality.

DWELLING IN THE SECRET PLACE OF THE MOST HIGH

Psalms 91:1,11-12 declares,

> "He that dwelleth in the secret place of the most High shall abide under the shadow of the Almighty . . . .for he shall give his angels charge over thee, to keep thee in all thy ways. They shall bear thee up in their hands, lest thou dash thou foot against a stone."

Again, as with the foregoing scriptures, we must approach this text with the understanding that ancient Afrikan symbolic language was highly developed and tends to mean something quite different than the infantile interpretations the present level of modern man's lack of understanding has reduced it to. Firstly, how does one dwell in the secret place of the Most High? The answer is simple. By going inside of yourself. Going inside yourself through prayer and meditation is probably the quickest way in which you can make contact with the Creator. Sages of the ancient Afrikan High Culture civilizations taught that this was the best method of attuning oneself with that "light which lighteth every man that cometh into the world" and that self-control in your thoughts and actions released the energy forces which align you with the Creative Power that brought you into being and the laws of nature which sustain your existence. So in essence, dwelling in "the secret place of the most High" denotes a quiet state of meditation.

Let us reflect on this for a moment. The wicked machinations of the enemies of the world and of our people in particular have so thoughtfully and skillfully, yet cruelly, all but totally accomplished the main thing they have been trying to do for centuries and that is to cut the Black Race off from the life giving source of that spiritual energy which once made us so great as a people and can make us great again if we set about the business of deeming it a priority to tap directly into the cosmic wellsprings of Divine Intelligence. This is what they have done among other things. The enemy has purposefully defined and fostered a culture among Black People which is so noisy, loud and boisterous that it induces the brain to lapse into a state of euphoria; a mode of conditioning wherein a person relinquishes the desire to think analytically about anything. The lyrics of most of the music and the incessant "on the one beat" constantly pumped into our communities is designed to appeal to the foolishness in our people. You may not like my saying this; nevertheless, it is true. Therefore, I appeal to you to transcend an emotional reaction to this reality and consider the fact that the white capitalist money moguls of the record and video industry make megabucks off of the huge proceeds from the sale of electronic ignorance to our people.

Now I know this is strong language and could be considered a value judgement, yet an intelligent observation of the present state of the race, especially many of our youth, can bring home certain realities. For instance, when you walk through most Black Communities, especially in the summer, what do you hear; noise, just about everywhere. This noise provides a constant impetus for agitation. Is there any wonder then why in the midst of this environment so many violent incidents are prone to erupt; a fight down the street, intermittent bickerings here and there, someone getting upset and blowing a minor infraction all out of proportion, something always keeping you in a state of flux. How often do you feel relaxed in many of our communities? Why even when you are behind closed doors in your own little secret place, many times your peace is disturbed by chaotic sounds from the external surroundings. Yet when you venture into the enemy's community, usually the environment is quieter and there is less agitation; you hear few sirens speeding through the neighborhood. As you peruse through communities where the people who presently run the world live, you hear quiet music; generally classical music; music that flowers can grow around and you can hear birds sing to; music designed to enhance an atmosphere conducive to balanced thinking.

Contrast this with the boogie boom boxes, blaring car radios and warfare mentality in all too many of our neighborhoods and you begin to understand what a thorough job the enemy has done. Nevertheless, there is a peace that you can opt to maintain within a given environment. For you can, of your own free will, create a healthy atmosphere for yourself and your family. To do this you must first be able to experience yourself before everything else gets a hold of you; therefore, you must come under the shadow of the protective wing of the Almighty. That is attune yourself with your Creator by taking some time out of each day to get alone and be quiet so you can make contact and communicate with your own thoughts, your own feelings and inner being. Therein is the beginning of wisdom and the strengthening of your ability to make the right choices and consciously be an example to help bring about the corrective changes so greatly needed in our communities on an individual as well as a collective basis. This is the true function of an angel.

The claims in verses 11 and 12, "For he shall give his angels charge over thee, to keep thee in all thy ways. They shall bear thee up in their hands, lest thou dash thy foot against a stone", if taken literally poses some questions to an observant and analytical mind. If the righteous devotees of various religious persuasions are protected by supernatural beings such as angels, how come innocent babies are being raped and abused in today's world? How could that happen if they are supposed to be protected? These are guiltless. Why are so many good people being killed as it is common knowledge today that "the good die young" which often they do in this violent world? Even some of the most devout Christians meet with horrendous deaths and I have seen many ministers at a loss as to how to try and explain this because the doctrine of most Christian denominations teaches that when you accept Christ as your personal saviour, you put yourself in God's hands and he gives his angels charge over you so that you don't even stub your foot on a stone. You don't even trip, let alone have a car accident. What happened then with the faithful who have experienced traumatic deaths? Obviously, the poetic utterances of the text is someone's imagination or symbolic language at work, for surely it cannot be taken literally especially when you consider the fact that there is the ethereal belief in Judaic, Christian and Islamic theology of the physical protection of guardian angels on the one hand yet we behold something quite different taking place in the tangible world around us.

Again, we hasten to add that it is not our intention to attack anyone's personal belief or religious practices. Nevertheless, these are questions which must be answered. I therefore suggest the logical answer and conclusion seems to be that the angels, birds and other protective winged creatures that we have seen depicted in various art forms and described in the Bible are figurative representations of the protective power of Divine Providence and Intelligence which can be evoked through a reverent positive mental attitude. For it is by careful precautionary measures applied to the best of your ability that you are relatively able to insure the safety of yourself and your family. Then after you have done the best that you can, you leave the rest, as the elders say "in the hands of the Lord".

In this regard we must call attention to one's mental attitude and aura emission as a key factor because the kind of aura you carry with you can either attract or repel danger. If you walk around in a fearful state, you will most likely experience that which you fear. There is even a scripture which quotes the biblical character Job as saying "For the thing which I greatly feared is come upon me, and that which I was afraid of is come onto me." And the book of Proverbs admonishes "The fear of man bringeth a snare . . ."[11] These passages of scripture demonstrate the fact that if you entertain fear, life will find a way to fulfill that expectancy for you. If you walk around in a phychosomatic state, you will more than likely experience illness. Mind you we're not talking about spookism here, but the science of aura transmission and electrical magnetism which operates on the same principles as does the electrical energy employed in the transmission and reception of audio and video waves one experiences through a radio or television set. In short, the type of vibrations you send out will inevitably attract the kind of energy forces you will encounter in your life. Esoterically speaking this is what the guardian angel principle represents. For it is through careful safety precautions and one's mental attitude and aura transmission that one can either attract or repel harm and danger.

Isaiah 40:31 seems to emphasize this point when it says "They shall mount up with wings as eagles". In other words, you shall be the one that transcends danger. You shall be the one who overcomes adversity in your life which means then that we are not compelled by any Divine fiat to accept a condition of life that is less than perfect. Of course, we know that perfect is relative. Yet we are to strive for perfection by doing our very best in all that we endeavor to do. This indicates that humans should look inside of themselves to link up with the Creator's protective power, not to some external supernatural mythological being. Why am I putting emphasis on this? Because often Black Folks are led to look outside of themselves for something or someone to do for them that which they can in fact do for themselves. Now I am not denying that the Creative Force in the cosmos is there to come to your aid when necessary, yet one has to take the basic responsibility for one's own life. Other than that you leave your whole existence to something outside of you which is a very unsafe thing to do.

Remember, ancient mythological symbolism was the technical language and scientific formulae of those times. Therefore, free yourself from the folly of believing the symbol of something to be the real thing. Also bear in mind that the most powerful deterrent to finding the solution to your daily problems is fear, anxiety and doubt. You should never allow fear, anxiety and doubt to govern your life. Actually, you should not allow these energy drainers to ever exist in your thought processes. Now we know this is easier said than done, but it is certainly worth the effort. For you can accomplish milestones in your life and maybe add some years to it as well by simply eradicating those three negative emotions; fear, anxiety and doubt. Especially doubt in your own worth and ability. This was the supreme object lesson of the ancient mythology of angels, to affirm the reality that one can transcend adversity and overcome life's obstacles through self-help and Divine Guidance. That's what all the angel stuff was about. Are we clear on that?

Approaching this from another dimension directly related to our daily lives, let us reaffirm that the protective winged creatures above the pharaoh's head and those with wings flanking his body, the angel hovering over Ur-Nammu in prayer and thousands upon thousands administering to the Ancient of days in Hebrew literature were usually portrayed as feminine entities and were ancient symbols of spiritual energy and power. Therefore, having a personal guardian angel signifies a positive mental attitude normally stimulated by the divine unity of Black Love. Yet even if a soulmate is not present in your life, you can still embrace the posture of self-motivation and transcendence. However, should you be blessed to share in the wonders of Black Love with a member of the opposite sex, when you are with your mate seek as often as possible to maintain a positive environment and even when problems and adversity arises assume the attitude of the divine black unity and friendship which originally drew you together and collectively seek a solution rather than focus on the problem or cast blame upon one another because of it. If neither of you are of a frame of mind to do this at the time, then recognize the fact that neither of you are the enemy; lovingly reaffirm your friendship, ask for Divine Guidance and set about the business at hand. In due time the answer will come and when it does you will surely understand that things were not nearly as bad as they seemed. So my beloved brothers and sisters, don't waste a lot of time being angry with your mate, but rather put that time to good use while you are in arm's reach of your guardian angel's powers for it is a gift from God.

2

ANGELS IN ANCIENT KEMETAN HIGH CULTURE

The concept of winged feminine protectors and revivers expressed in ancient Kemetan High Culture science is probably a carry-over from the Nubian-Grimaldi voluptuous Afrikoid figurines interred with the deceased between 20,000-100,000 years ago. These we will be discussing in Essay Seven. We have earlier cited that the Kemetan culture, in terms of its historical chronology, preceded the cultures of Sumer, Phoenicia, Arabia, Persia, India and Babylonia; all of which were originally Kushites. As the fledgling Hebrews who were of this same Afrikoid racial stock successively passed through the kingdoms and city-states of these great civilizations, many of the elements of these cultures were handed down to them. This is how the Israelite priests and scribes came upon the idea of winged spirits and angels exemplified in Isaiah 6:1-3, 6-8.

> "In the year that King Uzziah died I saw also the Lord sitting upon a throne, high and lifted up, and his train filled the temple. Above it stood the seraphims: each one had six wings; with twain he covered his face, and with twain he covered his feet, and with twain he did fly. And one cried unto another, and said, Holy, holy, holy, is the Lord of hosts: the whole earth is full of his glory . . . .then flew one of the seraphims unto me, having a live coal in his hand, which he had taken with the tongs from off the altar: and he laid it upon my mouth, and said, Lo, this hath touched thy lips; and thine iniquity is taken away, and thy sin purged. Also I heard the voice of the Lord, saying, Whom shall I send and who will go for us? Then said I, Here am I; send me."

Here the Prophet Isaiah is reputedly having a vision of the Creative Force sitting upon a throne; his royal robes filling the heavens and flanked by celestial beings with six wings called seraphims; chanting one to the other in praise to the deity. Keep this picture in mind because we will meet with a semblance of it again in the Kemetan text.

The terminology seraphim comes from the Hebrew root *sera* meaning "burning one" and the Hebrew word *seraph*-"a brilliant winged serpent". Literally "a burning serpent". Not an actual burning serpent in the strictest sense, but rather it denotes an aspect of the ancient science of the mind in which it was said at it's highest level of performance was stimulated by "the serpentine fire". The symbolic gesture of one of the seraphim touching Isaiah's tongue and lips with a fiery coal conveys the idea of fire purification which signifies kinetic energy force that touches the mind and the spirit. This fire is usually representative of the inspiration which comes from the Feminine Energy Force in the cosmos as is illustrated in the case of the *kundalini*, an allegorical type of the energy which moves up the spine to the medulla oblongata at the base of the brain. That force one feels when spiritual energy is motivating them especially in the "midnight hour" when you're with your mate.

The Afrikan High Culture scientist of antiquity believed that this spiritual fire could only truly be generated through a man's erotic experience with woman and if it were generated by anything else, it was not the right fire. This will become more apparent to the reader as we continue. The question may arise as to why I am putting so much emphasis on the female fire. I would respond by saying because the ancient wise men and sages did. Remember, their's was a High Culture Science, far exceeding that in the modern world today in terms of spiritual enlightenment and cosmic understanding. For they unequivocally understood that it was the female who first established the principles of elevated thinking and civilized behavior among men. She was the one who established an agrarian society, a family structure and out of that developed all of the other sciences of the world. That is why intimacy with the original Black Woman was referred to as "the serpentine fire".

So what is taking place in the Isaiah vision, though somewhat masculinized by the later male chauvinistic outlook of the Israelite ecclesiastical aristocracy who had adapted to and assimilated some of the values of the Eurasian nations in close geographical proximity to them, is in actuality a description of the feminine energy force in the process of enlightening the prophet: giving him knowledge and understanding: motivating him to say I will go and carry the message "Here am I, send me."

THE FIREBIRD AND THE SERAPHIM

The seraphim creature depicted in the Isaiah scroll is also related to the phoenix as the firebird is referred to in the Greek language.

This flaming emblem of immortality was known as *bennu* to the Kemetans. The *bennu* was a mythological bird said to live for 500 years, after which time it would kindle a fire on a brier of aromatic spices by fanning its wings, then become engulfed in the flames and perish. During this process a metamorphosis takes place and the firebird transfers life to a newborn phoenix who would then rise out of the smoldering ashes and soar to the sky, spreading the arts and sciences of civilization for another cycle of 500 years.

The Random House Dictionary of the English Language renders definition #4 of phoenix - "A person or thing that has become renewed or restored after suffering calamity, or apparent annihilation." Truly this emblem is indicative of the Black Race throughout the ages even unto this day where it has become the national symbol of the Provisional Government of the Republic of New Afrika. Dr. Chancellor Williams further elucidates this in *The Destruction of Black Civilization* as he delineates the many historical instances in which the high civilizations of the Black Race, after suffering devastating attacks from the Eurasian and Caucasian invaders, would move further south and build another magnificent civilization that would marvel and incite invaders to a vicious and destructive jealousy whenever they would, several hundreds of years later, venture to trespass in our lands again. Dr. Williams goes on to tell us that this happened repeatedly for untold centuries after our initial encounters with the relentlessly aggressive pale creatures from the north who first invaded the Mother Continent around 5,000-6,000 years ago. Our ability to repel most of those attacks and reconstruct after defeat is a testimony to our traditional greatness.

That is the real meaning of the phoenix. Afrikan People constantly rising again. The Black Race imbued with the fire of a vitalizing stimulating force and governed by an indomitable spirit. Therefore, my brothers and sisters, this brilliant symbol of Afrikan antiquity should say to us, never stop hoping, never allow your spirit to be broken, never cease striving for excellence, never stop building viable institutions that sustain and nurture—that ignite us to rise up and take our rightful place in the sun once again. For if we should ever get weary and allow ourselves to stop, the cosmic fire which brings ever renewing life to the world would cease to burn and be gone forever. So we must be ever vigilant in our pursuit to reclaim the joy and beauty of civilization. We must declare, as the Prophet Jeremiah, " . . . I can't quit! For . . . his word in my heart is like fire that burns in my bones."[12] As long as the fire is in your bones, you will struggle to create a better existence, a better life and "a better condition than man has yet known". This is our destiny. Therefore, as a people we should not give in to the degenerate elements of Euro-American culture. We should not allow our sacred Afrikan souls to be persuaded to adopt or be contaminated by assimilation into the white man's definition of who and what we should be. Even though they may be presently in control of this world, we must always be about the business of keeping in tune with those values which are essential to us; family, communal sharing, a sense of community, etc. All those things which make life worth living.

The *Webster Reference Dictionary of the English Language*, Volume 1 defines phoenix thusly, "A paragon, a person or thing of distinction or beauty". Surely, they must be talking about the Afrikan Woman. A good example of this is the Dance Theatre of Harlem's performance of *Firebird* by Igor Stravinsky; a superb offering indeed. Should ever you have the opportunity to see this production, by all means take full advantage of it. For it is a truly delightful experience, especially with Miss Stephanie Dabney in the principal role. Nothing short of gorgeous, she brings the firebird to life right before your very eyes. I get a wonderful feeling just thinking about it. Ahhh, the power and glory of the original woman; the Afrikan Woman.

Returning now to the basic context of our exegesis of the Isaiah text, we cite a quote from *Harper's Bible Dictionary*. "Seraphim—celestial beings, an order of angels who along with cherubim . . . were thought of as guarding the throne of God . . . .the exact origin and symbolic meaning of seraphim is uncertain; possibly they were derived from the serpentlike creatures of Assyrian mythology, symbolic of lightening. Or from the Egyptian 'guardian griffins'."[13] The above document introduces several other terms in reference to angelic beings; cherubims and griffins. Both of which we will be discussing in Essay Three. For now we will focus on the idea that the seraphims "were thought of as guarding the throne of God". First of all, this language has to be symbolic because the Creator does not need to be guarded by anything. Secondly, evidently these seraphims are symbols of protective forces held in such high esteem that they are even portrayed as guarding the throne of the One, the Creative Force in the universe. With this we get some kind of idea of how important this symbology of divine protection was to the ancient world and we shall soon be able to find out why and what this meant in practical terms. As to Harper's reference as to the uncertainty of where the seraphim symbol may have derived, we can positively state with much certainty that it comes from the symbology of ancient Afrikan High Science Astro-Mythology.

THE JUDGEMENT SCENE IN AFRIKAN SCRIPTURES

It is rather doubtful that those of us today who have been exposed to the vast body of Afro-centric information presently in circulation need be reminded that Kemet often misnomered Egypt was and is in Alkebulan (on the Afrikan continent) and that the large majority of its inhabitants were and are indigenous to it. As in "for real, sho nuff" Black Folks. For those who may not have been aware of this historical reality, now you know. The particular Afrikan scriptures made reference to in the above heading are texts from the Kemetan *Book of the Coming Forth By Day and By Night* misnomered *The Egyptian Book of the Dead* by many unenlightened Euro-centric Egyptologists.

The Hebrew concept of seraphims standing guard over the throne of the deity is directly transmuted from figures depicted in Kemetan judgements scenes, such as the one illustrated in Plate 2. In this setting we note Ausar (Osiris) sitting on a throne with one-winged creature fluttering above and before him and two women standing behind the throne with hands upraised and placed upon the deity as though bestowing some type of energy or power. There is much historical and scientific information set forth in this symbolic pageant, but time and space will not permit us to contemplate it here. In Plate 3, a portion of the same scene is exhibited with a close up view of the two women who are representations of Auset (whom the Greeks called Isis) and Nephthys. Auset is pictured with a throne on her head; the significance of which we will discuss under the next heading. Nephthys is crowned with an incense burner which denotes the spiritual awakening, insight and enlightenment she infused to the deity. In Plate 4, the same Ausar (Osiris) is covered by the wings of Auset and Nephthys. Now the picture becomes very clear. This graphic scene, drawn from the *Book of the Coming Forth By Day and By Night* was in circulation in the ancient world centuries, perhaps millenia, before the Hebrews incorporated it into their scriptual imagery.

The judgement scene that one now hears so much about in ecclesiastical settings is one of many mental images which the Hebrews embraced while they were in Afrika. The two Black Women, Auset and Nephthys, portrayed protecting the Pharaoh Auser under the shadow of their wings were archetypal matrices for the Phoenician, Sumerian, Babylonian, Assyrian and Israelite seraphim. These Afrikan Women were the original guardian angels.

Next we come to a scenographic enactment of the resurrection of Auser, the Kemetan Christ, and the three hawk manifestations shown in Plate 5. Auser's corpse is lying on a brier in the process of being resurrected. Auset is standing at his head. She is also represented in one of the three hawk symbols. The others are Nephthys and Het-Heru whom the Greeks called Hathor. Het-Haru is emblematic of a female entity which typifies the goddess of the sky, love, beauty and happiness. The resurrection of Auser is one of the first stories of a resurrected god ever depicted in human history. The characterization of the three birds with fluttering wings in the picture demonstrates the feminine forces. Auset, the animating power; Nephthys, the spiritual energy, enlightenment and prayer and Het-Heru, who represents love, beauty, joy and the essence of the celestial atmosphere. This is what it takes to bring a Black Man back to life. In plain language, the exalted interplay between the male and female principles is the key to a regenerated life. That, my brothers, is why the Black Man must have the one and only true angel in his life; the Afrikan Woman.

In the philosophic worldview of ancient Kemet, the pharaoh was protected by applying the wisdom of cosmic intelligence as manifested in the female spiritual energy. His growth and development in this knowledge and wisdom was largely dependent upon his bond and connection with the queen who through her affection, comfort and counsel perpetually fanned his mind and spirit with her loving arms, her gracious wings.

LAP OF AUSET, THE THRONE OF POWER

Let us here reflect on the sublime meaning of the throne symbol manifested in ancient Kemetan High Culture Science. Henri Frankfort informs us concerning the eat of power in the ancient Kemetan Empire " . . . the name of the goddess Isis is written as if it simply meant 'throne', while she is also depicted with the throne as her distinctive attribute . . . .the throne, Isis, is the 'mother' of the king . . . .The bond between the king and the throne was the intimate one between his person and the power which made him king . . . .The throne which 'made' the king is comprehended as a mother, and thus it may be the object of profound and complex feelings."[14] See Plate 6. Why is the throne connected with Auset (Isis), the mother force who stands behind the god Auser (Osiris) and/or surrounds him with her wings as she is also depicted standing behind and protecting all of the pharaohs of Kemet? Because they were said to be her sons. Why? Because she symbolizes the matrilineal system first developed by Afrikans; the line of descent through which the throne is inherited. Thus "the throne which made the king is comprehended as a mother and . . . may be the object of profound and complex feelings". Pharaoh Seti I is spoken of as reposing of the thighs of Auset (Isis) upon ascending the throne at his coronation (ca. 1321 BCE). See Plate 7.

In ancient Afrikan societies, the king's throne was referred to as his mother's lap because it is through the female line that he receives his power and the king was not the king until he had been annointed by the queen. For it was then ardently believed that it was only by the power of the female force that man had achieved civilization in the first place. Therefore, there would not be a nation if it were not for her. She established the whole concept. In retrospect, what appears to have occurred with the process of time, even though women ruled on the throne for long periods, in many cases women became weary of direct rulership as the Earth became less peaceful. So they opted to put most of their energies into cultivating the social systems that kept true civilization alive. At first in making this choice, women lost no real power because the man who ruled as a custodian of the nation was her son and could only rule by her consent. In those days she was the initial formulator of men's attitudes and social consciousness. She determined what the society would believe in, what they would fight for, and what they would strive to achieve in life. Notwithstanding the guidance of the males as father forces in the community, all this was basically implanted in the mind of the child through the inspiration of mother because most of the early impressionable years were spent with her. She was the nourisher, the first stage of inspirational motivation in a person's life. Even then "the hand that rocked the cradle ruled the world".

So today it is not by accident that Black Men have "profound and complex feelings" for their mothers and even refer to their wives and soulmates as Mama. It's an old Afrikan custom. Not that a man thinks of himself as a baby before his woman, but rather that he recognizes her not only as his woman and his wife, but his source of inspiration. The same as his mother was and probably still is to him. So when he refers to her as Mama, it is a very holy and sacred thing. It is indicative of the fact that your first comfort and the first woman you ever loved in life was your mother. So naturally that transference goes to your woman. She is unto you a mother, a sister, a daughter, a friend and a lover. As you are unto her a father, a brother, a son, a friend and a lover. You are to be to one another that "secret place of the most High", an oasis where you can find rest from a weary world.

Some of our readers may wonder why I keep placing so much emphasis on this. Well, it is because I believe that the realization and internalization of the historical reality of the Afrikan Woman's true role in the creation and maintenance of world civilization is a master key to the Black Race reclaiming and regenerating its traditional greatness. Personally, I grew up with a somewhat male chauvinistic outlook and when Dr. Yusef ben Jochannon and other Afrikan scholars began teaching this concept, it took me weeks to get it together especially when he informed us that man's first idea of a Supreme Being was Mother-God. As the saying goes this declaration "wasted me" and I walked around wrestling with it for several weeks. Then I returned to my studies in ancient Afrikan history determined to objectively research the subject thoroughly. As a result of that decision and positive action, I am now happy to say I have seen the light. For I have come to understand that when the Black Man assumes the proper attitude about the sacredness of the feminine energy of the Black Woman, he then brings himself back in line spiritually and as he sincerely demonstrates this in word and deed, the world will begin to respect him again and he will advance by quantum leaps toward taking his rightful place in the sun. For this primary purpose was the male entity created, to protect, defend, guide and provide for the woman and the children she bears. As he earnestly sets about doing this, she then is free again to be his nourisher and the inspirational force which motivates him and her to do great things. Herein, for Afrikan people, lay the secret of life's balance.

In antiquity, Afrikan Men tenaciously defended the matrilineal system with their very lives because as long as the woman was respected and held in high accord then the nation had dignity. After all when you can debase the mother of a people, that's the worst you can do to them. The matrilineal system did not diminish the male gender. Obviously the role of the male was and is very important. As he accorded her the respect and reverence as the Queen Mother of the universe, she in turn said to him because you put your life on the line for me and for these children and because you are the first line of defense facing danger without thought for your own safety, because you put us first, I now look up to you and confirm you in the position as king in my life. I do this because I want to and I will continue to do it as long as you respect me. So it wasn't that she served him or he served her, it was in fact a give and take situation. The role of the male and female was so clearly defined at that time that they could securely walk hand in hand, side by side, ruling the world together. Granted things are drastically different in this age, yet we can of our own free will reaffirm the correct attitude. As one song writer has said "there is no me without you".

In summation, the throne of the queen mother's lap represented the collective power of the Afrikan in the ancient world. So then today can the harmony and unity of Black Love help to restore us to our traditional greatness. For it is written "As it was in the beginning, the same shall be in the end". The scenography of Auser, Auset and Nephthys signifies harmonious activity between the masculine and feminine energies; generated by the love and inspiration that comes from the mother force. This is a potent object lesson sent to us down through the annals of time. A wondrous testimony to the original power and glory of our Afrikan Ancestors. Let us therefore pick up the torchlight and shine forth as the noon day sun for the throne of power awaits us.

3

SAFE AND SECURE IN THE WINGS OF BLACK ANGELS

Further investigation into the symbology of angels leads us to the subject of cherubim who were generally portrayed as protective forces of ancient Afrikan rulers. The terminology cherubim is from the Hebrew *kerubim*- "to hold steady" and the Chaldean *karibitu*-"to intercept danger". In terms of functional tangibility "to hold steady" means to keep a calm and steady head in the face of danger for by so doing you will be in a better position "to intercept danger" that is deflect or neutralize any perilous threat to your person and the well being of your loved ones.

GOD TAKES A CHERUB RIDE

In the Old Testament scriptures, we read,

> "And David spake unto the Lord the words of this song in the day that the Lord had delivered him out of the hand of all his enemies, and out of the hand of Saul: . . . In my distress I called upon the Lord, and cried to my God: and he did hear my voice out of his temple, and my cry did enter into his ears . . . .Then the earth shook and trembled; the foundations also of the hills moved and were shaken, because he was wroth. There went up a smoke out of his nostrils, and fire out of his mouth devoured, coals were kindled by it. He bowed the heavens also, . . . And he rode upon a cherub and did fly: and he was seen upon the wings of the wind."[15]

What in the world is this? Obviously a graphic use of poetic language. Firstly, the text states that it is "the words of a song". Secondly, it reveals that the poet was motivated by anguish. He was in trouble and called upon his god. The deity responded with fury; came down out of the sky; riding on a cherub and ignited the heavens causing the hills and valleys to shake and tremble in the manner of a modern day airplane bombarding a targeted area. What a vivid description. These are apparently the recorded emotions of a man who had just been engaged in carnal warfare.

Now, this is the same Bible that some folks say teaches us to be non-violent and turn the other cheek. Yet here this servant of the Lord had just come from bloodshed and saw God. Warfare had inspired him. Why? Because to him it was a righteous war. The principle being conveyed here is that in the ongoing conflict between the forces of good and evil, extreme measures are oft times necessary. As the scriptures say in another place, "There's a time of peace and a time of war". Whenever someone and/or something disturbs your peace many times the only way you can ever have peace again is to go to war. Thus this bible writer is describing a battle and to him in the midst of the carnage he could see the Creator being revealed; riding on a cherub; speaking with thunder clouds; surrounded by darkness and spitting fire.

CHERUBS IN ANCIENT BLACK CULTURES

The phycho-pictography of angels in the form of two-winged cherubs defending and protecting people and places was very much in vogue in the ancient world. We will first cite several examples from Hebrew culture, then demonstrate how the Israelite imagery was taken directly from the Kemetan. According to *Harper's Bible Dictionary*, cherubim also referred to as "living creatures" in Hebrew literature were depicted in Israelite symbolic mythology " . . . guarding the tree of life in Eden (Gen. 3:24): placed in pairs at each end of the mercy seat of the Tabernacle, protecting the sacred articles in the Ark (Ex. 25:18-22); embroidered on the veil of the Tabernacle (II Chron. 3:14); and sacred symbols in Solomon's Temple . . ."[16] Let us now focus on the Israelite usage of cherubim iconography in the construction of the Ark of The Covenent and the embellishment of Solomon's Temple. Hebrew scriptures tell us that Moses was instructed,

> "And they shall make an ark of shittim wood: . . . And thou shall overlay it with pure gold, within and without shalt thou overlay it, and shall make upon it a crown of gold round about . . . .And thou shalt make two cherubims of gold, of beaten work shall thou make them, in the two ends of the mercy seat. And make one cherub on the one end, and the other cherub on the other end: even of the mercy seat shall ye make the cherubim on the two ends thereof. And the cherubims shall stretch forth their wings on high, covering the mercy seat with their wings, and their faces shall look one to another; towards the mercy seat shall the faces of the cherubims be . . . .And there I will meet with thee, and I will commune with thee from above the mercy seat, from between the two cherubims which are upon the ark of the testimony, of all things which I will give thee in commandment unto the children of Israel."[17]

The Ark of the Covenent as it was sometimes called was a box overlaid with gold and had golden poles inserted through it lengthwise for carrying. See Plate 9. Only certain members of the priestly class in Israel were allowed to transport the ark from one location to another. Affixed atop the box was a flat golden disc called the mercy seat, a light known as the "shakina" was said to shine above the seat between two cherubims. Careful analysis of the materials used in the ark's construction as described in the Exodus scroll reveal that this sacred box of the Hebrews was actually a battery. Recently it has been reported that some students at Georgetown University reconstructed the ark according to the specifications of the Old Testament scriptures. After the students completed the project, the box generated such hazardous amounts of electrical voltage; they were ordered by school officials to dismantle it immediately.

The two angel-looking creatures, the cherubims with their wings touching at the top, we shall shortly meet again in the original Kemetan version of this iconographic style. It should be remembered that Moses was born, raised and lived on the continent of Alkebulan (Afrika) in the nation of Kemet for at least 80 years. There is where he was educated and there is where he was first initiated to the construction and science of the ark long before the Israelite nation was formed.

Edward Sugden demonstrates the correlation by informing us that in Kemetan (Egyptian) temples

> " . . . the central object of devotion was the sacred bark. This was a boat about eight feet in length. Upon the boat there stood a canopy or catafalque; and from this was suspended the square shrine of the god, hung by ropes, and kept from swaying by guide ties at the bottom. Some shrines had a winged figure of Maat, the goddess of truth, at each end, embracing the shrine with her wings. Such seems to be the prototype of the winged cherubs on the Jewish Ark . . . . the sacred ark of Amon-Ra at Karnak is carried by staves on the shoulders of twenty-four priests; and the shrine under the canopy is about three feet square, and shows the winged cherubs on either side. A small image of Ra is seen within the shrine. Moses discarded the boat, which represented the bark on which the sun god traversed the heavens daily, and its crew of minor deities; and for the image of Ra he substituted the two tables of the Covenent, or Testimony, which could not be mistaken for an image of Jehovah, but which symbolized His spiritual presence in His revealed Word. In its shape and material the Ark followed its Egyptian model, as well as in the arrangements for its transport."[18]

According to verse 22 of the Exodus text, the Lord God told Moses "I will commune with thee from above the mercy seat, between the two cherubims which are upon the ark of the testimony, of all things which I give thee in commandment unto the children of Israel." Is this text saying that the Supreme Creative Force in the universe which dwells in all the granites of the Earth, all the stars of the air, all the leaves of every tree, every grain of the sands of the sea was going to reduce itself and sit on a seat on top of a box? Or is it symbolic language for something else? We know in Kemet it was, but what was the intent of the Israelite scribes and priests who first set this story to writing for the subjugated Hebrew nation in Babylon around the 5th Century BCE.

No doubt seeing the top of a battery light up in the middle of the desert around 1240 BCE when the ark was supposed to have been constructed was indeed awe inspiring and conjured up in the minds of simple folks a sense of being in the presence of a supreme deity. After all few of them, if any, had privy to the same knowledge Moses had received from his Kemetan High Culture education.

Here the very same Bible, which teaches us God is a spirit which cannot be seen by man[19], tells us that the same Supreme Being used to hang over a golden box between images of angels and talk to the children of Israel to the exclusion of every other nation. In essence these people had reduced God to a boxtop and if you did not come and worship at their boxtop, you were out of luck. This is incredible; a paradox indeed. Undoubtedly, this is the work of some person or persons on an ego trip. Yet we see this same spirit demonstrated today in many institutionalized religions-the idea that the Creator will only meet with people in this or that particular church, mosque, temple or shrine. According to the egocentric fanatics of such dogma, God just won't meet with anybody anywhere else but in their houses of worship. This is sheer arrogance which serves neither the Creator nor man. How can you limit the Cosmic Force of the universe to a prescribed time and space? Mind you it is not my intent to attack anyone's personal belief, but logically speaking, how can mortal man confine the One, the Unmoved Mover, to pages in a book, to a graven image or a particular house of worship? Unless, as was the case with the learned priests of the Afrikan High Culture Systems, it is understood as a symbolic gesture.

Dick Gregory gives us a good example of Euro-Christian arrogance when he relates a childhood experience in which he says Catholic priests told him that Black People were cannibals in Afrika so white folks brought us over here, enslaved and Christianized us to keep us from eating each other up. Then they took him to

Holy Communion in the church; gave him some white wafers and some juice and told him to eat the body of Jesus and drink his blood.

Barbara Walker points out that from time to time there was much superstition about the Ark of The Covenent circulating among the Hebrews. On one occasion

> ". . . an ox cart, . . . teetered 'because the oxen shook it' and would have fallen, had not Uzzah 'put forth his hand to the ark of God, and took hold of it' (2 Samuel 6:3). In spite of Uzzah's good intentions, God instantly struck him dead for daring to touch the holy object. Again, when the ark returned from Philistia, God perpetrated an extraordinary slaughter of 50,070 well-intentioned people for daring to look inside the ark in their joy: 'and he smote the men of Bethshemesh, because they had looked into the ark of the Lord, even he smote of the people fifty thousand and three score and ten men: and the people lamented, because the Lord had smitten many of the people with a great slaughter' (1 Samuel 6:19)."[20]

These events, probably exaggerated, may have been written to relate some catostrophic event which had taken place because of the extremely high voltage of electrical current generated by the ark. Walker also adds that the terminology ark originally meant "great ship, metaphorically the Great Yoni: a female-sexual vessel bearing seeds of life through the sea of chaos between destruction of one cosmos and creation of the next."[21]

Twin cherubs facing one another and enshrouding pharaohs with their wings was a very popular emblem in ancient Kemetan symbology. In relationship to Kemetan and Hebrew similarities, the *Seventh Day Adventist Bible Dictionary* says, "Egyptian representations paralleled more closely the cherubim overshadowing the ark. In the tomb of King Seti I, two winged human shaped beings are represented, who looked at each other and spread their wings in such a way as to protect the god or king between them. Similar representations are found carved on temple walls and on shrines."[22]

If present biblical and historical records be correct, Moses attended school with Seti I's son Raamses II and while working his way up through the various levels of the Mystery System curriculum of which Moses only attained the level of a Hierogrammat—meaning he completed only eight of the forty-two books of Tehuti[23]—he learned of the significance of cherubim symbolism as it was applied in Kemetan High Culture Science. A science we are now rediscovering that was far more advanced than previously thought by some scholars.

One of the more elaborate Hebrew sculptural imitations of Kemetan rulers sheltered by the wings of cherubs is recorded in I Kings 6:21-29.

> "So Solomon overlaid the house within with pure gold: . . . And the whole house he overlaid with gold, until he had finished all the house: also the whole altar that was by the oracle he overlaid with gold. And within the oracle he made two cherubims of olive tree each ten cubits high. And five cubits were the one wing of the cherub and five cubits the other wing of the cherub: from the uttermost part of the one wing unto the uttermost part of the other were ten cubits. And the other cherub was ten cubits: both the cherubims were of one measure and one size. The height of one cherub was ten cubits, and so was it of the other cherub. And he sat the cherubims within the inner house: and they stretched forth the wings of the cherubims, so that the wings of the one touched the one wall, and the wing of the other cherub touched the other wall; and their wings touched one another in the midst of the house. And he overlaid the cherubims with gold. And he carved all the walls of the house round about with carved figures of cherubims and palm trees and open flowers, within and without."

The "oracle" spoken of in verses 21 and 22 is in reference to the chamber where the Ark of The Covenent, from which Yahweh is said to have communicated with the high priests of the children of Israel, was housed. The use of the term "oracle" as applied in the text gives us another indication as to the degree of esteem the Hebrews may have accorded the ark. An oracle is a person or place where people go to find out things; to get answers to their problems; to find out what the future holds in store for them. One of the most renown oracles of the ancient world was the shrine of the two Black Doves symbolic of two jet Black priestesses who came out of Afrika and settled in Greece when it was colonized by Kemet.

The size of the cherubims, "ten cubits high", with wing spans of the same measurement, given the cubit in the ancient world at the time of the writing of this text being about one and one-half feet, would make these huge statutes 15 feet high by 15 feet wide. From the description of this text, the Hebrew artist must have had quite a fascination with the Kemetan imagery of cherubims; illustrated by the manner in which they carved so many; overlaid them with precious metal and put them just about everywhere including the doors of the temple. (Verse 32).

We have previously cited artists conceptions as shown in Plates 4 and 10 which depict Ausar (Osiris), the first Kemetan pharaoh, engulfed in the wings of Auset (Isis) and Nephthys. This same concept is illustrated in Plate 11 without the wings and once again we come to the throne headdress of Auset which we have already discussed and Nephthys' headdress, an incense altar symbolizing the power of meditation and spiritual transcendence. Nephthys is also known as Nebthet, the new hope of sunrise, queen of the light and "Lady Day". These iconographs affirm the real meaning of cherubims. The idea of being safe and secure in the wings/arms of Black Angels.

Phoenician cherubs were usually sculptured in the forms of winged sphinxes. See Plate 12. Other "neighbors of Israel had symbolic winged creatures, such as winged lions and bulls, guarding the temples and palaces of Mesopotamia, and the Egyptian winged creatures in the temple of the Zodia of Dendar. Hittites had griffins-winged sphinxes having lion's bodies and eagle's heads and wings. Ezekiel's description of the 4 composite 'living creatures' (Chapter 10) seen by the River Chebar may reflect Babylonian observations."[24]

The four cherubim of Ezekial 1:10 are portrayed in association with the throne of Yahweh. Dr. John G. Jackson and Barbara Walker tell us that these figures represent the four seasons and the four cardinal points of the zodiac. The faces of the four "living creatures"; a human is the sign of Menat (Aquarius); the lion is the sign of Atum (Leo); the ox is the sign of Ausar (Taurus); and the eagle is the sign of Nephthys (Scorpio).[25] For other examples of cherubim imagery in the ancient world, see Plate 13.

EUROPEAN CORRUPTION OF CHERUBS

Sphinxes with eagle-wings called griffins were used in medieval architecture along with gargoyles also known as grotesques " . . . decorative figures in Christian churches, taken from the animal gods, masques, sirens, gorgons, satyrs, Green Men, serpent deities, and other idols in the sacred caves of paganism. Early churches were built right over the heathen 'grotto' and the same deities were worshipped side by side with Christian ones, so the people would continue to come to the church by force of habit, finding their familiar idols there . . . .to which people still prayed secretly, or touched for 'luck', . . ."[26]

Gargoyles and griffins are still used in many modern day structures to ward off evil spirits. This is a tradition that has been going on since the Dark Ages. In fact, many such Gothic images can be seen on buildings in major cities throughout the United States. Ugly vile looking creatures with their mouths hanging open were put on the corners of church building up into the 20th Century, an extension of the good angel-bad angel syndrome of Euro-Christianity. During ante-bellum slavery the same so-called "intelligent" people who were enslaving and exploiting Afrikans because they had to civilize us "primitive heathens" were constructing buildings with griffins; moreover, gargoyles to protect them against evil spirits. This clearly shows how some people's emotions can supercede reason. Surely the expense and effort invested in putting these creatures on top of buildings hasn't done much good because as a whole Euro-Americans are still acting evil towards Afrikan People in America and other peoples of color in the world.

In the European corruption of the feminine energies of the Auset and Nephthys principles of the Ausar drama, cherubs are depicted as little babes with wings in medieval and modern art. For example, Valentine cards with Cupid shooting arrows into the hearts of lovers. Yet the idea of cherubim goes all the way back to the ancient Afrikan concept of protective energies and the role of the female principle in the establishment of kingship.

Brothers and sisters, almost everything you see in this world, if you examine it closely, you will most likely find a reflection of yourself. Thus it is with the iconography of angels in the language and symbology of the ancient world.

4

SAPPHIRE EVE
DIVINE MOTHER OF THE UNIVERSAL EGG

SISTER SAPPHIRE: A JEWEL IN THE HEAVENS

One of the most graphic illustrations of a deity in the midst of celestial powers is the Prophet Ezekiel's vision as recorded in the Hebrew scriptures.

> "And above the firmament that was over their heads, was the likeness of a throne, as the appearance of a sapphire stone: and upon the likeness of the throne was the likeness as the appearance of a man above upon it. And I saw as the color of amber, as the appearance of fire round about within it, from the appearance of his loins even upward, and from the appearance of his loins even downward, I saw as it were . . . the appearance of the bow that is in the clouds in the day of rain, so was the appearance of the brightness round about. This was the appearance of the likeness of the glory of the Lord. And when I saw it, I fell upon my face, and I heard a voice of one that spake."[27]

Other than the obvious fact that the entity sitting on the throne is a Black Man—the color amber being that of a golden brown hue—the most distinctive detail in this word-picture is the throne itself. Understanding that all the imagery in this reputed revelation was allegorical symbolism employed to demonstrate a particular object lesson or set of values, the question arises in the minds of today's astute observer. Just what exactly was the meaning of the "sapphire throne" as adapted by the Hebrew scribes.

Firstly, the sapphire stone was a jewel of great value in those days and its ethereal blue color was symbolic of lofty thoughts, spiritual attunement and cosmic manifestations. In fact, it was the lapis lazuli used so prodigiously in Kemetan jewelry and artifacts. In Sumer and Babylon it was called the stone of the "Cosmic Mother". The name Sapphire is often used as a term of endearment by Afrikan Men today in reference to the spiritual energy and precious gift of the Black Female. Although at times the name has the dual purpose of at once describing the twin attributes of the Black Woman's sweetness as well as when she "gets her habits on" or as some brothers say 'get to acting evil'. But even when the name is applied to the latter it still generally engenders feelings of affection for the Afrikan Woman in the hearts of true Black Men.

Secondly, as concerning the throne, Erich Neuman observes;

> "As mother and earth woman, the Great Mother is the 'throne', pure and simple, and, characteristically, the woman's motherliness resides not only in the womb but also in the seated woman's broad expanse of thigh, her lap on which the newborn child sits enthroned. To be taken on the lap is, like being taken to the breast, a symbolic expression for adoption of the child, and also of the man, by the Feminine. It is no accident that the greatest Mother Goddess of the early cults was named Isis, 'the seat,' 'the throne,' the symbol of which she bears on her head; and the king who 'takes possession' of the earth, the Mother Goddess, does so by sitting on her in the literal sense of the word. The enthroned Mother Goddess lives in the sacral symbol of the throne. The king comes to power by 'mounting the throne,' and so takes his place on the lap of the Great Goddess, the earth—he becomes her son. In widespread throne cults, the throne, which was originally the godhead itself, was worshipped as the 'seat of the godhead'."[28]

This concept of the throne as the dwelling place of the godhead is awesomely reaffirmed in Ezekiel's vision when he refers to the enthroned golden brown image as "the appearance of the likeness of the glory of the Lord". The throne (lap) of the woman's body was also revered by the ancients as being simultaneously a holy symbol of "earth" and "paradise" (heaven).[29]

Regarding the designation Eve as used in the title of this chapter, Rosalind Jeffries informs us that in the Hebrew analogies as found in the book of Genesis, the name translates into "Giver of Life" or "Mother of All Living".[30] We will be focusing on other aspects of "Eve" further on in this essay, but at this point, let us lend our attention to the meaning of . . . THE DIVINE MOTHER OF THE UNIVERSAL EGG.

THE EGG: A UNIVERSAL SYMBOL OF NEW LIFE

Universally the ancients viewed the egg as the archetypical symbol of world creation and affectionate encounters with woman. Afrikan Women were earthly manifestations of the Divine Mother of all creation, and union with them was perceived as experiencing the divine vessel of life especially in the case of sexual expression. In many old cultures, the egg represented the new life that returns to nature each spring. It was " . . . a representation of the old cosmic egg, the universally known symbol of the primordial matriarchal world, which as Great Round contains the universe."[31] We find this symbol in modern day spring festivals such as Easter. Even though in this case the original meaning has been misconstrued. Though many ancient cultures associated the rabbit which represented the moon with the egg, they certainly did not portray this totemic symbol as producing them as did the Germans who used to tell their children that the hare would lay eggs for them if they were good.[32]

The moon's influence over the birth cycle which involved the full maturization of the fetus produced from the fertilized female egg and the sympathetic harmony of its phases with the female menstrual cycle was observed by Afrikan High Culture scientists as having a natural correlation. Motivated by what Godfrey Higgins called "the egg of wisdom",[33] the ancient Kushite and Kemetan scientists observed through their investigation that the female reproductive cells or ovum of animals gave rise generally only after fertilization to a new individual or another living being. Thus the great respect for the egg and its universal symbology as an emblem of creation.

The concept of the cosmic egg is a feature of many Creation stories. The myth of the universal world egg was and is known throughout Alkebulan, among the Hindus of India, in the old cultures of Greece, China, Japan and the isles of the South Pacific. "In these myths, creation is symbolized as breaking forth from the fertile egg. The egg is the potential for all life, and sometimes, as in the myth of the Dogon people of west Africa, it is referred to as the 'placenta of the world'."[34] " . . . the people of early ages worshipped the genius of fruitfulness, not only among human creatures, but also in all things that were capable of reproducing, and condemned, aye, cursed sterility or non-production." To them the serpent represented organs of generation as did the bull in Kemet and "fertility was symbolized by the egg . . . "[35]

THE EGG AS A SIGN OF THE SACRED FEMALE VESSEL

Not only, as Neuman relates in his book, *The Great Mother*, was the egg in one of its aspects symbolic of the moon, it was also in Kemetan hieroglyphics to denote the roundness of the Earth.[36] The Persians, who like other nations in Mesopotamia received their science and culture from the Kushite-Kemetans, believed the Earth had hatched from a giant egg which was their symbolic way of explaining the 360 degree principle as it pertained to the orbits of the planets in our solar system. These ancient Black astromoners, in their observations of the celestial elliptical orbits, identified them with the elliptical shape of the female vagina and ovaries. In fact, Kemetan " . . . signs for the World Egg was the same as an embryo in a woman's womb."[37] Other Kemetan designs " . . . presented even more overtly sexual hieroglyphics: downward-pointing phalli alternating with narrow mandorlas (female almond shapes), each topped by a small triangle representing a clitoris."[38] "This symbolism was held so sacred that its desecration was held punishable by death. The female organ of reproduction was emblemized by a unit, a circle, a boat shaped shell, a lozenge, or any object, animate or inanimate, that resembled these figures, or implied receptivity, fruitfulness or maternity."[39]

Believing that "the egg contains within itself the seed of all things", the master teachers of the ancient world often began their rituals of initiation into the higher mysteries by leading their neophyte students in a solemn ceremony known as the consecration of "the eternal egg".[40] At one time in eastern Europe, people used to place red colored eggs on graves to serve as resurrection charms.[41] This practice is reminiscent of the Nubian-Grimaldi who buried their dead with voluptuous Afrikoid female figurines all over Europe about 40,000 years ago. In olden days eggs were always symbols of rebirth as well as being associated with new birth which was considered to be the prerogative of the female gender.

The role of the woman as the "sacred vessel" was expressed and depicted in a multiplicity of ways throughout the ancient cultures and high civilizations whose priests kept carefully attended holy pots and golden urns in their temples and sanctuaries to denote the every present reality of the feminine productive and nurturing powers. To find heaven, obtain wisdom and effectuate oneness with the cosmos, they taught, a man must know the divine experience of spiritual, mental and physical unity with the woman, an achievement which they called *maithuna*.[42]

The main character in the modern day Mother Goose fairy tales is an extension of the age old "universal egg" philosophy. "Mother Goose originated in ancient Egypt, where she was Mother Hathor, incarnate in the Nile goose. She laid the Golden Egg of the sun, another way of saying she gave birth to Ra. His solar disc was sometimes called the Goose-Egg. Some Egyptian writings called the goose Creatress of the World because she produced the whole primordial World Egg."[43] That "World Egg" was in fact the womb of the original Black Woman, the divine Queen Mother of the universe.

EVE, THE MOTHER OF ALL LIVING

The code name "Eve" as applied in scientific circles represents probably several thousand Black Women who shared the same gene pool about 200,000 years ago and possessed a particular strand of mitochondrial DNA. An article in *The Black American*, Volume 27, No. 3 carried the headline ALL FAMILY TREES LEAD TO 'EVE', AN AFRICAN SCIENTIST CONCLUDE. The reporter, Boyce Rensberger, goes on to clarify the declaration thusly,

> "The claim is not that 'Eve' was the only woman having children 200,000 years ago. She had many contemporaries who were each among the ancestors of many living today . . . .all of today's racial differences evolved after descendants of Eve had grown quite numerous and migrated out of Africa into Eurasia. The differences arose after various populations of the descendants had become geographically separated . . . .the findings suggest that while there were primitive forms of homo sapiens living throughout Africa, Europe and Asia, fully modern humans arose in only one small population in one place and their descendents eventually spread throughout the old world, replacing the earlier populations . . . .the conclusion that Eve lived in Africa emerged from comparing the amount of difference between every possible pairing of individuals among 147 persons tested from all over the world, . . . ".

The January 11, 1988, issue of *Newsweek* displayed an astonishing cover which portrayed a Black Man and Woman in the Garden of Eden with the title THE SEARCH FOR ADAM AND EVE, SCIENTISTS EXPLORE A CONTROVERSIAL THEORY ABOUT MAN'S ORIGIN. Following are some highlights from that article accompanied by comments from this author.

> "The scientists Eve - subject of one of the most provocative anthropological theories in a decade-was more likely a dark haired, black-skinned woman, roaming a hot savannah in search of food . . . .she was not the only woman on Earth, . . . she was simply the most fruitful, if that is measured by success in propagating a certain set of genes. Hers seem to be in all humans living today . . .".

Thus we see that ancient Afrikan scientists were not off base when they taught about the "universal egg"as representing the womb of the original Black Woman.

> "When scientists announced their 'discovery' of Eve last year, they rekindled perhaps the oldest human debate: where did we come from? They also, in some sense, confirmed a belief that existed long before the Bible. Versions of the Adam-and-Eve story date back at least

> 5,000 years and have been told in cultures from the Mediterranean to the South Pacific to the Americas. The myth makers spun their tales on the same basic assumption as the scientists: that at some point we all share an ancestor. . . . what's startling about this Eve is that she lived 200,000 years ago."

Imagine this, over 200,000 years ago a group of Black Women became the genetic mothers of the whole world. In other words, the planet Earth was peopled from the extension of the original "sacred vessel"; the Afrikan Woman's womb. The contemplation of this fact should give today's Black Woman an idea of who she really is and inspire the Black Male to accord her the respect she is properly due. Just understanding this in all its ramifications and internalizing it accordingly will help to make the Black Man a better man, a stronger man, an insurmountable being of eternal spiritual stamina and power.

> "Most evidence in so far indicates that Eve lived in sub-Saharan Africa . . . the evolution from archaic to modern homo sapiens seems to have occurred in only one place, Eve's family. Then, sometime between 90,000 and 180,000 years ago a group of her progeny left their homeland endowed apparently with some special advantage over every tribe of early humans they encountered. As they fanned out, Eve's descendents replaced the locals, eventually settling the entire world."

Note the reference to this most ancient group of Afrikans who began populating the "entire world" about "90,000-180,000 years ago" who were endowed with "some special advantage over every tribe of early humans they encountered" and bear in mind that there were no Caucasians of any kind in existence at that time unless you accept the theory of the Neanderthals as being their archaic ancestors and even then from about 100,000 -35,000 BP when the Neanderthals died out they were not caucasoid. As has already been stated, there were no white people anywhere on Earth before around 20-25 thousand years ago and here you were in the person of your Afrikan Ancestors traveling the world "endowed" with a "special advantage" some 200,000 years ago.

> "To find Eve, Rebecca Cann first had to persuade 147 pregnant women to donate their babies' placentas to science. The placentas were the easiest way to get large samples of body tissue. . . . Cann selected women in America with ancestors from Afrika, Europe, the Middle East and Asia. Her collaborators in New Guinea and Australia found Aboriginal women there . . . .all the babies DNA could be traced back ultimately, to one woman."

DNA is the code initials for deoxyribonocleic acid, the chemical of which genes are composed. The major factor in the genes—genes being the basic unit of inheritance—which determines what a being will be. That is to say DNA is the hereditary material of living cells. Mitochondrial DNA is inherited only from the mother and it functions as a cells power house converting the chemical energy from food into a form which the cell can use. Rensberger says "this special kind of inheritance—we all get our mitochondrial from our mothers—makes it possible to come to this kind of conclusion". The mitochondrial Eve of 200,000 years ago was the common ancestor of all humans. For an artist' conception of mitochondrial DNA and how it functions in the human cell, see Plate 14.

> "The Berkeley biologists conclude that everyone outside Africa stems from a group of Eve's descendents who left their homeland between 90,000 and 180,000 years ago. As they moved across Europe and Asia they would have encountered Neanderthals and populations of archaic homo sapiens, they were probably outnumbered in many places. But wherever the daughters of Eve went, only their mitochondrial DNA survived .... the fact remains that the Neanderthals mitochondrial genes all disappeared after Eve arrived so both the Berkeley and Emory biologists suspect there was little or no mixing maybe the immigrants were so different they couldn't interbreed. Or maybe they simply shunned the natives as being too 'primitive' the Neanderthals attempts at courtship presumably suffered if as some scientists speculate they lacked modern human's power of speech."

Now these were some for real "sho nuff super sisters" and like many Black Women if you don't have the rap, you can't get in the lap. That is to say with Sapphire you must at least be able to adequately express yourself in order to demonstrate your sincerity so you can imagine that Neanderthal Man, who probably couldn't talk at all beyond "ugh" and "uh", didn't stand a chance. Can't you just picture and hear a sister with her hands on her Hottentot hips and shaking her head while talking to some Neanderthal about 90,000 years ago saying "honey, you can't get nowhere here cause you just came out of your mouth with the wrong thing".

The article concludes by stating "Since we are all descended from Eve's daughters, any common male ancestors of theirs would be a common ancestor of everyone today." Of course common sense buttressed by mountains of cumulative data makes it very plain that this common male ancestor was a Black Man.

5

RHAPSODY FOR THE GLORIOUS QUEEN OF HEAVEN

PRELUDE

Because of their absolute adoration of the Afrikan Woman, ancient Afrikan Males, as do their descendents today, spent much time rhapsodizing "rapping" to and about Black Women, their glorious beauty and attributes. One of the main reasons being the fact that this woman increased his life span by minimizing the occupational risk of survival incumbent in the hunt for the Afrikan Woman was " . . . the first to plant and harvest crops, breed animals, spin and weave, and make pots . . .". The most important step from the semi-nomadic hunter-gatherer stage to the more sedentary stage of agriculture and the activities related to this occupation provided the basic foundations for investigative science and learning for each evolutionary step towards "civilization" was directly tied to man's stomach. This may have been his main impetus for invention, seeking new and better ways to feed himself. The most outstanding constituent who brought a high degree of deliverance for man from the hazardous domain of an ax-swinger and a spear-thrower and pointed him in the direction of being multi-faceted in the survival game was the creator of agriculture; the Black Woman. Yes, I'll say it again. It was the Afrikan Woman who, through the seminal science of the Earth-agriculture, set the stage for humanity's quantum leap from the hunter-gather, semi-barbaric level to the solid primary plateau of civilization. That is why she was hailed in olden days as "Mother Earth". Titled so because of man's gratitude for her role in the most important advance in the march towards civilization.

Woman the primary mother was also dubbed "Queen of Heaven" because she was associated with the rain that nourished the seed and its crops. The sun was revered as the father of the heavens because of its potent role in crop production.

"To the Original Black Man and most people of color a solid family structure was the most sacred entity in the world. The African male had a strong affection for women and children and his exalted view of the Black Woman was based on her particular place in the development of civilization. Therefore, the Black Man repudiated his primary duty to protect her, the children she bore and the society she nourished."[44] Diop adds "Moreover this situation has been unchanged since ancient times: the couples to be seen on the African monuments of Egypt are unified by a tenderness, a friendship, an intimate common life—the like of which is not to be found in the Eurasian world of this period: Greece, Rome, Asia. This fact, in itself, would tend to prove that ancient Egypt was not Semitic . . . "[45] For more information and discussion concerning ancient Black Male/Female relationships and their relevance to today's world, we suggest the reading of *Afrikan People and European Holidays: A Mental Genocide*, Book II pp. 20-27 by this author.

DIVINE BLACK MOTHER OF THE UNIVERSE

Every movement of nature in the cosmos, celestial and terrestrial, was associated with the life-giving, nurturing and sustaining principle of the Mother Force. That is why her worship was so universal. " . . . the forms assumed by this Great Goddess in the different parts of the world . . . are innumerable . . . If we survey the whole of the symbolic sphere determined by the vessel character of the Archetypal Feminine we find that in its elementary and transformative character the Feminine as 'creative principle' encompasses the whole world. This is the totality of nature in its original unity, from which all life arises and unfolds, assuming, in its highest transformation, the form of the spirit."[46]

In point of fact the "Holy Ghost" as mentioned in the New Testament scriptures is in actuality the feminine aspect of the primal Trinity; father-mother-child. There is even reference in the Christian text to this entity as being the "comforter whom I shall send". In the ancient world, even for adult males, the arms and bosom of the female was the most secure and tranquil place on Earth. This idea was later co-opted and corrupted by the early women hating church fathers of the Third and Fourth Centuries. In their editing of some of the original text, they intended to totally obliterate the exalted view of the female principle which was so prevalent in the ancient world. This kind of attitude was not unusual for the "sexually ambiguous" and "maladjusted" European for many of them were probably closet, if not blatant, homosexuals who were envious of the female principle. However, through some strange turn of history, the veneration of the Madonna and Child, who in essence were Auset (Isis) and Heru (Horus) of ancient Kemet, was salvaged in the Catholic Church whose theologians otherwise generally portrayed women as "the gateway to hell".[47]

This misogynistic posture on the part of European males was in stark contrast to early man's portrayal of the virtues of womanhood. Rosalind Jeffries reminds us, "The image of the primal mother goes back to early antiquity . . . .Some works show her as Primal Mother Creator, with fertilizing and nurturing powers which extended from the firmaments down into the earth below. Her powers of fertility in the universe were not confined to human beings but could be magnified to affect vegetation, animal husbandry, and the atmosphere. . . . Woman was the 'Giver of Life'."[48]

WHY THE IDEA OF THE GREAT MOTHER WAS SO IMPORTANT TO PRIMORDIAL MAN

> "Ancient societies believed that those related by mother-blood shared a common soul, so no member of the group would hurt another without doing injury to himself. . . . Mutual trust was maintained exclusively among members of a matrilineal kinship group known as 'mother's milk'. Societies where women set the standard of behavior and morality were found generally kinder than male-dominated societies. Children grew up without harsh punishment, expecting kindness from others as a matter of course and consequently developing into non-hostile, non-violent adults. Envy, greed, and exploitiveness were minimal; depression almost unknown; crime almost unheard-of. People were generally good-humored, trustful, and confident. Women were treated as the equals of men. Attitudes toward sexuality tended to be positive and permissive. People seemed to feel sure Mother Nature would provide for their needs, even in cases where a harsh environment demanded hard work for the sake of survival."[49]

In those life-enhancing societies, the original Black Man believed that Motherhood was expressly linked to superior intelligence and magical powers for they were keenly aware of and appreciated the fact that the time a child spent with its mother had a direct bearing on its cognitive formulation. All over the Earth life was measured by this "fundamental symbolic equation ... Woman=body=vessel=wisdom=the world".[50] This was a "universal symbolic formula" for early man because the first and most profound world that a human ever knew was that of his/her mother's womb. Then once delivered into the temporal world by her, his/her early life's experience was overshadowed by her maternal protection, nurturing, instruction and discipline. Understanding this, the first of all mysteries, I am totally in agreement with Dr. Yusef ben Jochannon when he says that motherhood is "still the most profound example of Godhood on earth".

For the Afrikan, the maternal instinct has always been of paramount importance. "From earliest times in Afrikan society there has always been a strong bond between mother and child. In our High Culture Societies, to show disrespect to one's mother is tantamount to sacrilege. To the Afrikan the maternal instinct is the primary basis for a civilized society and provides the impetus to the paternal instinct which enables a man to see himself as more than just an ax swinger and a spear thrower. This attitude on the part of Blacks in the ancient world generated their very high regard for the Black Woman as the Queen of the Universe."[51]

A perfect example of this Afrikan philosophy of life is illustrated by Cheikh Anta Diop in *The Cultural Unity of Black Africa*.

> "The Ashanti consider the bond between mother and child as the keystone of all social relationships. They consider it as a moral relationship which is absolutely binding. An Ashanti woman will not stint in the work she does or the sacrifices she makes for her children . . . .no demand is too exaggerated for a mother to meet. Although she shrinks from inflicting punishment and never disowns her child, an Ashanti mother requires from her children both obedience and affectionate respect . . . to show disrespect to a mother is equivalent to committing a sacrilege."[52]

And I might add in some societies a wayward child even as a fully matured adult would be hunted down and killed by its mother if that person did not cease doing that which was disrespectful or shameful to the community. We hear this attitude reflected in the Black Community today, "I brought you into this world, and I'll take you out", when mothers and fathers are admonishing their children who have wandered onto a wayward path.

In the societies established by the Afrikan in the context of his own creative and historical reality, there was no such thing as the teenaged crime and violence which often plague many Afrikan communities in America today. That is because these societies were tempered with a love and discipline that would not permit its members of any age to get that far out of hand. Granted, these were collective societies generally untarnished by the vicious spirit of Eurocentricity that now permeates much of the Black Community; nevertheless, we must not in our time acquiesce to this anarchy. Rather we must rise up and take a bold stand upon the sure foundations of the old positive values, reclaim our communities and either draw our children back to ourselves or put them in check. As Brother Malcolm said, "By any means necessary". Failure to do this would be a dereliction of our parental obligations and an affront to Almighty God and our Afrikan Ancestors.

Returning now to our original trend of thought, Drusilla Houston reminds us, "The spirit of the Kushite was to honor and to exalt woman, therefore, lineage was thus traced."[53] In those days as is often the case today, the mother force was the one thing you could always depend on. Even if you did not know who the paternal parent of the child was, there could be no doubt as to who was the maternal one. This may be one of the reasons why the worship of mother and child became an ageless practice in the ancient world. Vestiges of the Mother-God syndrome are still evident in Roman Catholic Marianity though in their pathological state of "ambiguous sexual dimorphism" the major emphasis is placed on the male, the son.

THE BLACK WOMAN AS MOTHER CREATRESS AND RULER OF THE EARTH

" . . . in Egypt (Kemet) not only was the ancient Goddess Nut known as the heavens, but . . . most astonishing of all was the discovery of numerous accounts of the female Creators of all existence, divinities who were credited with bringing forth not only the first people but the entire earth and the heavens above. There were records of such Goddesses in Sumer, Babylon, Egypt, Africa, Australia and China."[54] For thousands of years maybe even millions, all over the world the Afrikan Woman was portrayed as Mother Creatress and " . . . personified as the world-protecting, feminine, maternal side of the Ultimate Being, and as such , stands for the spontaneous, loving acceptance of life's tangible reality." She was the supreme revelation of "Existence-in the material cosmos" and she represented "all things made of matter and perceptible to the senses."[55]

Touching on another aspect of this same theme, Dr. John Henrik Clarke says,

> "I feel that there is a need to call attention to the historical status of Afrikan women and their contribution to the development of Afrikan societies, in order for them to be better understood as Warrior Queens in defense of their respective nations. The Senegalese writer

Cheinkh Anta Diop has shown new insight into this subject in his book *The Cultural Unity of Black Africa.*

He observed that most non-European societies are, mainly, matrilineal, the line of descent being traced through the mother. Dr. Diop extends the explanation this way: 'it is matrilineal and it is the man who brings the dowry to the woman'. This proves, if proof is needed, that the women in these old societies had respected rights. Most of these societies developed before Europe was born.

In Africa the woman's 'place' was not only with her family; she often ruled nations with unquestionable authority. Many Afrikan women were great militarist and on occasion led their armies in battle. Long before they knew of the existence of Europe the Africans had produced a way of life where men were secure enough to let women advance as far as their talent would take them."[56]

Barbara Walker thinks that "for a long men feared to oppose women because they were convinced women were more closely allied with the forces of nature. West African tribesmen testified that 'women were more powerful than men, for to them alone the mysteries of the gods and the secrets of things were known'."[57]

Dr. John G. Jackson sheds more light on this line of thought by stating that " . . . in the human race, before the rise of civilization, female rule was practically universal . . . .in primitive human society, the woman formed the ruling class; and even the male dominance of a later age was probably brought about through sexual selection on the part of females."[58] Probably one of the reasons why the patrilineal system gradually displaced the matrilineal system even in parts of Alkebulan is because of the incessant battles brought into our land by invading Asians and Eurasians. Because of his natural physique and brawn the protection of the community and the field of warfare became largely the arena of the Afrikan Male. Add to this the fact that he was fighting soldiers from a male dominated society where masculine authority figures were viewed with the most respect and one can kind of get an idea as to how the warrior-king became more and more dominant in the society and in many cases supplanted female authority. Of course I'm certain the causes for the transition from the matrilineal to the patrilineal system in many Afrikan societies were far more complex than that, but these may have been some of the basic reasons. However, for the most part, and I would say among the largest percent of Afrikan People, the male claimant for the throne had to come through the female line. Herein the Great Mother Creatress continued to maintain her cosmic dominion.

EVERLASTING SCULPTURED FORMS OF THE MOST BEAUTIFUL WOMAN ON EARTH

The original Black Woman was the first model and standard of feminine beauty. She represented the epitome of graciousness. The sublime elegance of her corn-rowed or bushy hair, the dignity of her facial comeliness with her broad nose and delectable full lips and the awe inspiring curves of her voluptuous form was the subject of artists all over the world around 40,000 years ago. In the cave paintings and various art mediums of the Nubian-Grimaldi and other Afrikoid groups, the Black Woman is portrayed in every walk of life including leadership roles such as warrior queens, master hunters, high priestesses and community officials as well as the traditional roles she created as healer, agriculturalist, animal domesticator, home maker, teacher and socializing community sustainer. Because the Nubian-Grimaldi culture had been so widely diffused, Afrikoid figurines of the Primal Mother have been found from Zimbabwe to western and eastern Europe[59] and they represent examples of the most ancient sculpture of the human form yet rediscovered.

In 1909, in lower Austria, a "Venus" figurine was unearthed of the type that was buried with the deceased about 20,000 years ago to help them make their journey to the spirit world. Commenting on this LeGrand Cleage says, "In the case of Grimaldi artwork, the truth stares across 400 centuries and reveals the African features of the people so skillfully depicted." And he continues by quoting Boule and Vallois.

> "In almost every case the head is scarcely blocked in; the hair is often represented, sometimes by simple parallel lines, . . . as at Willendorf, [Austria] . . . we can interpret this feature, also found in primitive Egyptian art, as a type of hair dressing, an arrangement in narrow plaits, or in short tresses or short tufts, such as are found in modern Negro or Negroid races, particularly of the Bushmen and Hottentot tribes whose hair is grouped in little bunches."[60]

In my unenlightened childhood days, we used to tease girls with a short crop bush and call them "pepper heads." Lord, am I glad I have since learned better for I have been "born again" to my true Afrikan self and have had the sacred privilege of affectionately caressing the natural softness of a sister's short-cropped bush on many glorious occasions in my life and each time I have said as have many other brothers "All praises due the Creator for the Black Woman" and now in my eldership years as I review portions of my life in pleasant reflection, I can truly understand why the Nubian-Grimaldi was so enamoured of this particular feature of feminine charm in his day.

In their artistic creations, the Nubian-Grimaldi put much emphasis on the divine manifestations of the Afrikan Female anatomy; breasts were the milk of life and the pillows of comfort, the amply endowed hips and posterior was one of the most remarkable signs of beauty in the ancient world and the vagina was viewed as the portal of heaven, the Garden of Eden, the gateway to new life. All of these things were very sacred to the original Black Man.

SIGNS AND SYMBOLS OF THE PRIMAL MOTHER

Why did woman become the dominant symbology of life-giving elements in the ancient world? No doubt because then, as now, all men knew that it was their mother's loving care which carried them for 40 weeks, birthed them and kept them alive in their early stages of introduction to life. That is why they developed such a wide variety of expressions of her manifold attributes. In this section we are only able to cover a few of the more noted signs and symbols of the Feminine Force. Here is how early homo sapiens from about 200,000 years ago and especially the Nubian-Grimaldi of 40,000 years ago probably perceived of evolutionary geology and human development.

> "Chaos and night, primordial water of primordial sky, earth, mountain, and stone-and then living things began to grow. Everywhere vegetative life is born out of this depth and darkness of the nocturnal beginning-as plant and tree, as star and herb. In the earlier stage of human life, the gathering of plants, roots, and tubers was among the main tasks of women, just as hunting belonged to the province of man. Through this intimacy with the plant world, the woman of the primordial period possessed a wealth of knowledge concerning this sphere of life which plays so essential a role in the primordial mysteries of the Feminine."[61]

In those remote times every aspect of life, everything that man could conceive as well as that which appeared as supernatural was thought to be in some way connected with the mystery of birth and the extension of the woman's role in the planting and harvesting of the food crops which fed the people and kept them alive. Thus in their understanding of the world that then was it was through the central navel of the maternal principle that all natural phenomena was interactive. Mother was the bread of life, the milk of renewed strength, the one that not only fed you but clothed you as well, for though that which father would bring home from the kill of the hunt was received in reverent gratitude, it was the products from the ground and the home spun thread of the weaver's loom that seemed to be most dependable and consistent. The hunt could take anywhere from a few hours to weeks or many moons, but the stored staples of the earth and the provisions of livestock was right there—in the here and now—ready for consumption. The Primal Mother was " . . . everywhere the ruler over the food that springs from the earth, and all the usages connected with man's nourishment are subordinated to her. She is the goddess of agriculture, whether its products be rice, corn or wheat, barley, tapioca, or any other fruit of the soil. For this reason the Great Goddess is frequently associated with a vegetable symbol: in India and Egypt with the lotus; as Isis, Demeter, or later the Madonna with the rose. Flower and fruit are among the typical symbols of the Great Mother . . . "[62]

HORN OF PLENTY AND COW OF HEAVEN

An Afrikoid figurine excavated at Lausses (Dordogne-France) held the horn of a bison in her right hand; a distinctive symbol of her domesticating powers.[63] Animal horns held in the palms of many of the prehistoric statuary and the " . . . horns on the image of Hathor and Isis, goddesses of vegetation, agriculture, and fertility . . . " are symbolic of the Mother Force's healing powers for Black Women were the first doctors and used these horns as containers for medicinal herbs and as a symbol of her creation of agriculture and animal husbandry as well as her role as "protectress, preserver and domesticator of animals."[64]

We can be fairly certain that various species of the animal kingdom were greatly relieved at the move on the part of man from a strictly hunter/gatherer subsistence to that of agricultural staples.

Strange as it may seem, in those days, for a woman to be called a cow was a compliment rather than an insult. Personifications of the Primal Mother were called the "sacred heifer" because the cow was " . . . the symbol of prolific generations and of intellectual nature. She was sacred to Isis in Egypt; to Khrisna in India, and to an infinity of other gods and goddesses personifying the various productive powers of nature. The cow was held, in short, as the personification of the Great Mother of all things, both of the mortals and of the gods, of physical and spiritual generation of things."[65]

Again the original Black Woman was also associated with the primal sea, moisture and rain, the sky and the firmament (Earth's atmosphere) because the life giving fluids of her body i.e. breast milk and the water sac which kept the embryo and fetus safe and warm and the vaginal fluids which bring comfort and paradisiacal joy to man, in short, most everything that makes life worth living for man is in someway embodied in the Afrikan Woman. Oh, if she could only come to know who she really is, many of the problems that beset Black People today would be overcome and solved. For I do truly believe, as do many of my colleagues, that the Black Man's recognition and acceptance of this historical and cosmic reality would make him a bolder stronger man, able to take on any challenge of life that he might be confronted with. This is indeed one of the master keys to solving the mysteries of life at this level of self realization. Think on that.

The term "heaven", as used in the English language, comes from the German word "himmel" which also means "mountains of heaven"-a reference to the Himalaya Mountains in Asia.[66] The idea "mountains of heaven" goes back to the ancient systems of symbology wherein mountains were identified with the life giving and nurturing qualities of the female anatomy as for instance the Mountains of the Moon in east Alkebulan were called the breasts of the Great Mother. Walker says

> " . . . the Nile was supposed to emanate from the Mountain of the Moon . . . beyond Ethiopia. This was one of the universal female-symbolic images in mythology: the lunar mountain, located in a garden of paradise, containing a great cave or labyrinth, producing the rivers of life. Its genital connotation could hardly be overlooked. Arabs called it Jebel Ka-Mar, the Mother-mountain. Even in medieval European romances it was the source of wisdom; . . . The genital metaphor of the mountain is still suggested by the (French) word mons meaning both a mountain and a female genital."[67]

In ancient times the embrace of and lovemaking with woman was referred to as "taking it to the mountain top" which in turn meant "ascending to the heavens". That is one of the reasons why in the literature of antiquity so many songs and poems were written to and about the Afrikan Woman and her heavenly charms.

6

BLACK WOMAN: *THE PRIMOGENIAL BIRD OF PARADISE*

The association of the Afrikan Woman with "heaven" resulted in her being totemically depicted as a bird because her influence with her children and her husband was at times ethereal inspiring them to do great deeds. As a matter of fact, the misogynistic European Christians, who mistranslated the New Testament scriptures, sought to conceal the fact that the Holy Ghost represented the Female Principle in the cosmos and the real meaning of why it was depicted as descending like a dove upon the head of Jesus at his baptism.[68] Again Walker informs us that the Latin word " . . . aves meant both 'birds' and 'ancestral spirits', or ghosts, or angels." And she goes on to tell us that, "The Chinese said women knew the secret of flying before men did. The Emperor Shun first learned it from two princesses. 'Down to a certain date the source of magical power lay in women . . . an indication of an ancient Chinese matriarchy.' In northern Europe also, the Goddess Freya owned all the magic feather garments that enabled magicians to fly though the air like birds."[69]

This idea was once universal. In fact, today the British still refer to women as birds. Although in most cases, for less that elevated reasons. In the ancient mythologies, the Afrikan Woman was called the "bird of earth", the "great mother" that laid the egg and at other times when the cosmic egg had hatched she was referred to as a "bird of heaven" that rises from it as the golden hawk.[70]

Throughout the ages the spiritual wings of the Black Woman has always ignited the soul and fanned the fires of human imagination. This feminine wisdom principle was the impetus for man's quest to drink from the fountain of eternal knowledge and the unction which spurred him on to accomplish most of the incredible achievements of the ancient Afrikan High Culture

Systems and civilizations.* That is why she is often depicted as the "serpentine fire", the Hindu reference to the energy force which moves up the spine and inspires the brain.

On the other hand, in her manifestations as Mother Nature, the earth with which the original Afrikan Woman was associated can also be violent and destructive as well as nurturing and sustaining in the process of bringing about change. In this role the scientific mytho-symbol was a vulture. For as all things come from Mother Earth, all material things return to her bosom in death. Jeffries tells us that "One of the oldest symbols associated with woman was the symbol of the vulture, the scavenger bird who lives off decayed or dying matter."[71] The symbol of the divine vulture which was quite prevalent in ancient Kemet denoted the fact that woman could salvage just about anything in the animal and vegetable kingdom and make it a palatable sustaining staple, especially in times of great adversity such as drought etc. This fact was well demonstrated by Black Women during antebellum slavery who turned the garbage of hog guts into a delicacy called "chittlins. Although she should be applauded for this stroke of culinary genius now that the worst of the storm has passed over and for health reasons that are quite obvious we need to cut the "guts" aloose.

Further touching on the vulture image as applied in ancient times, it must be kept in mind that the symbolism used to illustrate these principles were those of a highly sophisticated and complex science developed by Afrikans whose meanings transcend modern man's understanding in his present state.

Many of the Primal Mother figurines which personified fertility, voluptuousness and rebirth that have been exhumed from the grave sites of men and women have arms which transform into wings. For the original Black Woman was the first being to be identified with angels. The ancients believed she was the connecting link between heaven and earth. The intermediate between time and eternity. She was the first divine messenger of the cosmic godhead, the source of light and wisdom called Ma'at in ancient Kemet and "wisdom" in the Hebrew scriptures.[72] We will be discussing this with much detail in a forthcoming work by this author entitled *Afrikan Genesis III: A Narrative Commentary on the First Book of the Bible.*

* For additional information on the incredible scientific achievements of Afrikan Peoples in the past, read *In The Beginning was the Black Race* by this author and *Blacks in Science: Ancient and Modern* edited by Dr. Ivan Van Sertima.

TYING THE KNOT AND WEAVING THE THREADS OF WISDOM

Today we refer to marriage as tying the knot. In ancient times this meant that the union of male and female and the setting up of home and family life was the beginning of wisdom. That is because the people of early civilizations believed one of the elemental keystones of their progress was the ability to work and plan beyond the rugged individualism of former stages of human development and that having a family forced a man and a woman to think beyond the limits of personal sustenance. Out of this familial necessity, they felt, was born new creations and inventions.

The idea of the wisdom knot began first with the Black Woman because the initial responsibility for the child was hers. Thus it was she who first built the house, the village, the schools, created the market place and established laws and systems of governance. Therefore, she became the throne of power from which men ruled. The knot symbolized bringing knowledge and wisdom together in a unified focus to achieve a specific objective. Tying the knot once meant working cohesively to get something done. In the case of home and marriage to perpetuate new life in the world.

Our Afrikan Ancestors, in their natural mind-set and original level of exalted spiritual understanding, believed that an individual should not be permitted to get married until they had achieved and demonstrated certain degrees of wisdom as well as acquired the skills which enabled them to take care of themselves and their dependents. Thus, they would be a blessing to, instead of a drain on, the community. For this the young men and women were adequately prepared through successive stages of teaching and practice as set forth in the Rites of Passage secret societies, many of which still exist on the Mother Continent today.

From all available data it appears that the Primal Mother was the creator and founder of institutionalized education. Therein she was associated with the attribute of wisdom. "Can't you hear the voice of wisdom? She is standing at the city gates at every fork in the road, at the door of every house. Listen to what she says; . . . For the value of wisdom is far above rubies: nothing can be compared with it. Wisdom and good judgement live together, for wisdom knows where to discover knowledge and understanding . . . .I, Wisdom, give good advice and common sense. Because of my strength, kings reign in power. I show the judges who is right and who is wrong. Rulers rule well with my help . . . the Lord formed me in the beginning before He created anything else . . .

Whoever finds me finds life and wins approval from the Lord."[73] So says the Bible.

Jeffries provides us with some Afro-centric commentary on this text.

> "The Queen Mother's ancient scepter was called Nyansa Pow a staff with a 'wisdom knot' tied in its center. These are seen today on older gold weights. It is interesting that the Greek goddess Athena was the goddess of wisdom and she too was born on African soil and a knot was associated with her wisdom. The Libyan goddess of wisdom has her hands symbolically veiled and the cloth drawn up into a knot with long strands flowing from the knot. The Tuareg women and some descendents of the Garamantes continued the custom of veiling the hands with knotted cloth at marriage ceremonies where they sing for the newly wed bound or knotted in matrimony."[74]

Though the Greek version of the story says that Athena, the goddess of wisdom, sprang into the world from the head of Zeus, whom the Greeks initially called Ethiop. The original Kushite version of this symbolic fable was somewhat different. They say that Ma'at entered the mind of Amen-Ra, (the Greek Zeus), and inspired him with the ideas of creation. The Ma'at-Athena principle of the tale typifies that at the early stages of a man's development in the ancient world it was his mother who taught him everything he knew and even in his adult life there were the "oracles" presided over by the high priestesses who were consulted for counsel at times of critical decision making.

Portrayals of the original Afrikan Woman often depict her wearing a mask which signifies the special relationship the female principle has with the Cosmos and her privileged access to its mysteries. She was granted this exalted status because it is only the feminine gender that has experienced the power and pain of giving birth; this was of special importance to the people of antiquity because it was the primary means of perpetuating and nurturing the human species. The man planted the seminal seed, but the woman nourished, sustained and delivered it. Thus her most honored place in the society. She was regarded as the cosmic glue that held all things together.

As concerning woman's mystic role as the "cosmic weaver", Neuman says,

> "The primordial mystery of weaving and spinning has also been experienced in projection upon the Great Mother who weaves the web of life and spins the thread of fate . . . the tissue woven by the Feminine in the cosmos and in the uterus of woman is life and destiny

'reality' is wrought by the Great Weavers, all such activities as plaiting, weaving, and knotting belong to the fate-governing activity of the woman, who, . . . is a spinner and weaver in her natural aspect. The crossing of the threads is the symbol of sexual union—we still speak of a crossing of animals and plants—and the crossing of the sexes is the basic forms in which the Archetypal Feminine 'weaves' life."[75]

THE SACRED TEMPLE OF THE BLACK WOMAN'S BODY

Since "the natural elements that are essentially connected with vessel symbolism include both earth and water." And " . . . the maternal water not only contains: it also nourishes and transforms, since all living things build up and preserve with the water or milk of the earth. Since the water can be symbolically related to the breast as well as the womb . . ."[76] And since the feminine fluids are essential elements of life giving nourishment the body of woman was viewed as the sacred temple of heaven. Neuman elucidates this further,

"For obvious reasons woman is experienced as the vessel par excellence. Woman as body-vessel is the natural expression of the human experience of woman bearing the child 'within' her and of man entering 'into' her in the sexual act. Because the identity of the female personality with the encompassing body-vessel in which the child is sheltered belongs to the foundation of feminine existence, woman is not only the vessel that like every body contains something within itself, but, both for herself and the male, is the 'life-vessel as such', in which life forms, and which bears all living things and discharges them out of itself and into the world. . . . in addition, it is the nourishing vessel that provides the unborn as well as the born with food and drink. Only when we have considered the whole scope of the basic feminine functions—the giving of life, nourishment, warmth, and protection,—can we understand why the Feminine occupies so central a position in human symbolism and from the very beginning bears the character of 'greatness'."[77]

Further commenting on the esoteric symbology of the female anatomy, Neuman says,

"The Great Goddess as a whole is a symbol of creative life and the parts of her body are not physical organs but numinous symbolic centers of whole spheres of life. For this reason the 'self-representation' of the Great Goddess, her display of her breast, belly, or entire naked body, is a form of divine epiphany."[78]

KUSHITE-KEMETAN SCIENCE OF THE DIVINE MOTHER

In ancient Kemetan High Science symbology, the matter of primal Earth called Ptah emerged as the cosmic egg in the form of a great mountain from the primeval ocean called Nun or Nuni. Originally, this symbol in part represented the sea water-like chemical composition of the female womb. Nun is said to have contained within it the male and female energies and united them to create all other things and creatures. Walker says that Nun meant "fish" and it is related to the word "nonne" which means " . . . a nurse, because in antiquity priestesses were practitioners of the healing art."[79] Dr. George G.M. James tell us that "Atomic energy originates from water and earth, since water H_2O, and uranium, an indispensable ingredient in atomic energy, is found in the bowels of the earth."[80] Water is invariably linked with atomic power, the basic source of locomotion on planet Earth because atoms and molecules are the prime elements found everywhere in everything. We will be discussing this further in a forth coming work by this author *Afrikan Genesis: An Historical Reality* in the chapters dealing with the Memphite Theology which is the basis for all science and learning in the world today.

Neumann presents another dimension of the primeval waters in mother symbolism.

> "The pre-Christian plunge bath signifies return to the mysterious uterus of the Great Mother and its water of life. The plunge bath, which in Judaism has retained its ritual significance down to the present day, became in Christianity the baptismal bath of transformation that, as a late work of art still shows, is a return to the primordial egg of the beginning."[81] See Plate 15.

In ancient Kushite-Kemetan space science, they used the cosmic rhythm of the female body and the phases of the moon as the basis for reckoning time. Jackson says, "At an extremely early date, a connection had doubtless been observed between the 28-day cycle of the moon and the menstrual cycle of woman, and between changes of the moon and ocean tide."[82] This was the beginnings of the lunar calendar and as far as we know the first calendar. As the Kemetan astronomers continued to observe the roundness of the heavenly bodies, 2 days-symbolizing the duality of the masculine and feminine force-were added to the 28 day month making 30 days so that at the end of the 12 months the calendar would fulfill the 360 degree cycle-circle of all things. After further investigation they created the 365 day calendar year to synchronize with the journey of the golden orb of our solar system. There is a very interesting story of how and why the god Tehuti added the 5 days and created the solar calendar which again is directly connected with the birth cycle. We will recite and analyze this very interesting tale in *Afrikan Genesis II: Black Gods in the Land of Eden* by this author.

Concerning the Kushite and Kemetan understanding of time and space, Hunter Adams, III says,

> ". . . to the ancients, space was of life-and-death importance. We know this because all over the earth stand their mysterious, megalithic monuments tuned to the rhythm of the stars, cycles they realized were the pulse of life. Through exacting long-term observation, our ancestors determined that seasonal cycles, vegetation growth cycles, and even animal migrations and mating cycles correlated with the cyclic changing position of the moon and sun. That information provided them with a reliable and perpetual time frame-a calendar-to schedule their societal festivals and rituals and to know the optimum planting and harvest times. Their culture, along with their economy, was wedded to the sky."[83]

Very early on in their scientific development the original Black Man observed the cosmic correlation between the celestial cycles, agriculture and the female anatomy. Neumann points out that

> ". . . the Feminine is also the goddess of time and thus of fate. The symbol in which space and time are archetypally connected is the starry firmament, which since the primordial era has been filled with human projections . . . . whether—as in Egypt, Babylonia, Arabia, India, China and America—the heavens are interpreted as originally, according to the primordial twenty-eight stations of the moon, or as later, according to the twelve stations of the sun; and whether animal or plant, stream or ocean, are the dominant projections. The essential point is that each one of these projections was experienced as a part of the life of the Great Goddess, who bears and encompasses all things."[84]

The ancient Kushite and Kemetan scientists profound knowledge of the cycle of the circle gave impetus to the invention of the wheel which first began as the agricultural wheel for milling grain and as an implement for water powering machinery. All over Egypt (Kemet) and Ethiopia (Kush) today can be seen images of Khonsu (Ptah) " . . . depicted as a potter . . . forming the Egg of the world upon a potter's wheel which he works with his foot . . . .in the act of forming man from the matter—Earth."[85] Of course, the egg symbolized the womb of woman, the wheel-her vagina and Khonsu/

Ptah, the spermatozoon, the male planting seed in the body of the cosmic clay of Mother Earth which was synonymous with the Primal Mother.

All the signs and symbols of the scientific and religious world in ancient times grew out of their understanding of the cosmic union brought about through the divine inter-relationship between the masculine and feminine energies.

Houses, villages and cities were first built in the round as an extension of the mother's womb such as Great Zimbabwe whose ruins are still standing in the modern day Afrikan nation of Zimbabwe. In fact, the Kemetan word for house was the same as that used for mother. Quoting Lederer, Walker says, "In Egyptian hieroglyphics, 'house' or 'town' may stand as symbols for 'mother', as if to confirm the similarity of the individual and the collective nurturing function. In line with this, the more primitive structures-houses, rooms, tombs-are usually round ones . . ."[86] Diop tells us that the term *Ker* equals house, in Egyptian [Kemetan]," and is related to the word *per*. He goes on to add that,

> "The worship of Isis was evidently widespread in France, especially in the Parisian basin; temples of Isis, in Western parlance were everywhere. But it would be more exact to say 'Houses of Isis,' for in Egyptian these so-called temples were called Per, the exact meaning of which in ancient Egyptian, as in present-day Wolof is: the enclosure surrounding the house. The name 'Paris' could have resulted from the juxtaposition of Per-Isis, a word that designated certain cities in Egypt . . ."[87]

Rogers corroborating this historical example of the universal rhapsody to the Black Woman says,

> "It should be noted that Isis, pattern of wifehood and motherhood, was the first Madonna . . . The worship of Isis spread through the remainder of Europe and into Asiatic Russia. Ancient statuettes of her have been found in Northern France, in the Rhineland, and on the Moselle. Her temples were in all that region, as well as in Britain. She is believed to have had a temple in Paris and another nearby, at Melun. By certain archaeologists the word 'Paris,' is supposed to be a corruption of 'Bari-Isis,' becoming through Roman pronunciation 'Parisii,' the name of the tribe that inhabited the site on which Paris now stands. The boat in the coat-of-arms of the city of Paris is supposed to be the barge of the Negro goddess for Isis was the goddess of navigation, as will be seen later on."[88]

A fitting conclusion for this essay is summarized in the following fashion by Rosalind Jeffries.

". . . we have observed the woman in a great variety of styles and roles—the woman as primal mother, as giver of life, as virgin, symbol of purity, yet as destroyer, serpent and vulture, blessed rainmaker, herbalist and healer, warrior of Amazonic fierceness and power, protector of man, huntress and dancer, ringed and horned, wigged and hatted, veiled and masked. The Afrikan woman portrayed" [in ancient times] "indicates that, although her role is often distinctive from that of man and very various, it is a diversity flowing within a very structured communal system, and the woman is never insulated in a vacuum, removed from man or god."[89]

7

THE ROLE OF ANGELS IN THE LAST RITE OF PASSAGE

About the middle of the 18th Century, European anthropologists, paleontologists, archaeologists and some other "ologists" while digging around in Grimaldi, Italy near Menton, France came across a startling rediscovery. They found some very beautiful aesthetically formed Afrikoid statuettes buried in graves of the deceased. These statuettes which European scholars misnomer Venuses were clutched by the decedents to their breasts as they lay in a fetal position. A close examination of the skeletal remains revealed them to be in fact Afrikan in physiognomy.

The reason why these detailed sculptured figurines of voluptuous Black Women were buried with the deceased, especially males, is because in those days between 100,000 and 20,000 years ago, it was believed that the feminine energy had a direct contact with the netherworld; that is heaven or paradise. As Dr. Yusef ben Jochannon has clearly explained so often and in so many ways, "Man knew nothing about heaven until his mother's womb. That's the first heaven he ever knew anything about. When you come down the fallopian tube and are delivered into this world, you have just left heaven and that is why a man, if he is in his right mind, spends the rest of his life trying to be 'born again', trying to go back to paradise as often as he can." During that period of world history, Afrikans in Europe and around the globe who practiced this burial custom had the understanding that the Black Woman was a messenger to the heavens. That is why many of the statuettes exhumed had wings attached to them.

One of the aspects of the rite of passage from life on this Earthly plane to the return of one's being to the cosmic elements of the eternal forces was again symbolized by the wings on some of these figurines which in essence denoted a philosophic view propagated throughout the ancient world from time immemorial. The poetic belief that at the point of death the soul was embraced and borne by angels to an estate of eternal blessedness. We find this concept prevalent in many religious ideologies.

For example, one of them which comes to mind is the Islamic doctrine that members of the faithful who died during the course of a Jihad would straightway enter paradise and be received by 72 virgins. No wonder Muslims were prone to fight so tenaciously in battle. The idea that those faithful to Allah would be rewarded with beautiful Afrikoid daughters of paradise at death was first incorporated into Islamic theology by the Abyssinian Hadzart Bilal ibn Rahab.[90] This particular tenet of the faith was often used by Muslim generals to spur their troops on to victory. The promise of voluptuous Black virgins of paradise oft times proved to be one of the best strategic policies in the history of human warfare.

The women of Zululand used a similar incentive to inspire Shaka's warriors through suggestive dance movements and with the words of their songs they would remind those about to go into battle of the joys of erotic bliss they would receive if they were diligent and proficient in their defense of the nation.

The Ashanti women while menacingly tapping the ground with clubs and spears told their men outright that if they retreated from the battle ground in fear and returned home defeated, they would in turn maim and kill them. This prompted the Ashanti warrior while contemplating warfare to declare "If I go forward, I may die. If I go home, I will die. Better I go forward and die with dignity." That may have been one of the reasons why the Ashantis of west Alkebulan were one of the last indigenous nations to fall in the face of European colonial expansion.

Returning now to our discussion of the Afrikoid female figurines, we think it of primary importance to mention the fact that these and other excavated artifacts dating around this period from 100,000-20,000 B.P. were created by the inhabitants of the region in which they were found. Available scientific data indicates that these people were Nubians who journeyed from southeast Alkebulan to distant places like Italy, Spain, France, Portugal, Britain and Russia among other geographical locations. At the time of their first arrival in Europe somewhere between 100,000-40,000 years before the present, there were no white people to be found on the continent or anyplace else in the world. Therefore, the accomplishments of this particular branch of Afrikans cannot be attributed to any other race for there were no other races in existence on the planet at this time.

Euro-centric scholars have attempted to accredit the Cro-Magnon, the first leucoderm—that is the first people without color—with the creation of the artistic works of Nubian-Grimaldi civilization, but any well informed scientist knows that the Nubian-Grimaldis preceded the Cro-Magnon in Europe by at least 75,000 years. Cro-Magnon, the immediate progenitor of the white race, did not appear on the scene until between 20-25,000 years ago. Prior to this Black Folks had been roaming the Earth for well over one million years. Further scientific investigation reveals that Asian peoples evolved ca. 15,000 years ago as the result of some Afrikan and Caucasian cross-breeding.

The descriptive terminology Nubian-Grimaldi is preferred by this writer because Nubians from the Mother Continent are what these people in fact were and because Grimaldi, Italy is where the first specimens were unearthed in recent times. Anthropologists generally label them just plain Grimaldi which is an incomplete reference. These Afrikans were stunningly beautiful people; dolichocephalic (long headed) with robust bodies. The steatopygia (ample posterior) of the women was a hallmark of great beauty and literally worshipped throughout the world in those days. In fact, this particular feature of Afrikan female physiognomy is still held in high esteem by brothers today. Just watching a Black Woman stroll down the street has caused a many aware Black Man, including yours truly, to moan Umh-umh-umh, Lord have mercy! Surely the Afrikan Woman is a joy to behold in all her aspects.

In the ancient world the physical symmetry and spiritual essence of the Black Woman was not only associated with the complex systems of beliefs and ritualistic burial ceremonies of the last rite, but the Queen of the Universe as she was then revered deeply influenced the other rites of passage as well. Her connection with the rite of birth was obvious for you could not make your journey to Earth without her. For thousands of years Europeans thought the act of procreation was solely the prerogative of the woman. They didn't have an inkling of an idea of the male seminal role in the process. On the other hand Afrikans of antiquity clearly understood that even though the seed may be planted by the male force, it is the female who is the only one that has the cosmic equipment to nurture and maintain for 40 weeks of gestation that which was to be brought forth in the newness of life. Afrikans were so enthralled by this cosmic miracle they evolved an entire body of scientific knowledge based upon its observation.

The rite of passage pertaining to the secret societies of manhood and womanhood training designed to prepare the youth for the lifestyles and responsibility of adulthood were definitely influenced and probably initiated by the mother force for she was the one who first established social order in homo sapien communities.

In the marriage rite, when the unifying partners received the collective permission of the community to set up housekeeping to return to paradise and be born again—good God Almighty—in this respect the Afrikan woman's sweet "Honey, I love" inspirational role was certainly firmly established.

So potent was the Black Woman's function in the sum total of life that the pharaohs of Kemet had themselves buried with images of her in the form of Nuit, the Sky Goddess, painted or engraved on the inside of the lid of their coffins so that she could vicariously lay upon him for all eternity. See Plate 8.

In many cemeteries today one sees statues with wings representing angels. We are told that these angels are neuters. They are neither male nor female. Now that might be the case in the European world, but in the Afrikan world, we didn't and never really wanted to know about anything but female angels. The Afrikan Woman was the only one associated with the birds in the sky.

To our Ancestors the Black Woman was Mother Sky, Mother Earth, Mother of Everything and she had the power to, through her spiritual essence, move freely throughout the universe. They believed that man could only reach the pinnacle of his spiritual being through her. I know some insecure brothers may not like to hear this, but if you are spiritually attuned and your manhood is intact, then you will understand. And you will do, like our wise Afrikan Ancestors, you will fight to the death to defend her honor because that's where your source of power and strength comes from.

I would now remind my beloved Black Sisters that a positive, optimistic loving woman strengthens and gives life to a man, but an antagonistic, negative or pessimistic one can destroy him. The same applies to brothers in relationship to sisters. Yet in the final analysis, it is the woman who determines what type of treatment she will receive and accept from a man. She is the one who can ultimately inspire him to be a real man because whether he relates to her in the role of a father, brother or lover, he is always her son. This was the way of the ancients.

AFRIKAN CONCEPTS OF DEATH AND RESURRECTION

The basic outlook of Afrikan People in regard to passing from this life to the eternal ethers is that we never viewed death as a finality. We never saw it as the end but rather a transition from this terrestrial stage to some other type of existence in the universe. To some this attitude may appear to be spookish, but not so if you understand the physical sciences. Atoms and molecules are never destroyed in the process of metamorphosis. They merely become parts of other things, other substances. Thus it is with human expiration. Many of the elements which composed our Ancestors live on in us and will continue to abide in us until we ourselves in turn become ancestors.

Some Afrikans who once dwelled on this Earthly plane performed deeds and had spirits that were so magnanimous their presence can still be felt by many people in many places. Oft times simultaneously. The life force of personages of the caliber of Fannie Lou Hamer, Dr. Martin Luther King, Jr., El Hajj Malik El Shabazz (Malcolm X) just to mention a few will always be alive in the ethers around us as they perpetually speak to the hearts of the people. Okomfo Kofi Boakye corroborates this scientific reality in the following manner. "The universe moves in cycles and mankind is compelled to move with it. Our Ancestors studied the cycles of the universe and developed a profound understanding of how we move with these cycles. Human beings go through a cycle of birth, procreation, death and rebirth. We are born. We have children. We die and we are reborn."[91] Now when one begins to understand this he or she will have no fear of death because you will come to realize that death is not final.

For some creatures on this planet who were not a part of the original energy which issued forth from the cosmos and who tend to function primarily on a material plane death may be the absolute end and perhaps they would be justified in fearing it, but for the Afrikan, this is not so. Some folk may not approve of my making this statement; nevertheless, it is real. Those of my people who are still in doubt as to the validity of this perspective, I suggest you read *The Iceman Inheritance: Prehistoric Sources of Western Man's Racism, Sexium and Aggression* by Michael Bradley who is himself a caucasian.[92]

One of the most ancient and sacred beliefs of the Afrikan regarding what is misnomered death is that man was not merely biological, that humans were more than physical beings. Ancient Afrikan High Culture scientists understood from the very earliest periods at the dawn of civilization that human beings were a composite of many elements and that the mental and the spiritual aspects of a person were as essential, if not moreso, to his/her existence as the physical. Thus the harmonious development of the mental, the spiritual and the physical well-being became the highest priority in the educational objectives of the old masters.

The great thinkers of the original Black Race also conceived of he grave as the bosom of Mother Earth. This idea was directly related to the belief that the force of Mother Nature in the cosmos possessed the powers of life (birth) and death—that the force which brought you here is the force you would return to. Therefore, in her aspect as Mother Earth, the Feminine Force, was the grave which opened her bosom to receive the body of her child back to eternity whom she one day would bring to Earth again through the birth of another. So even though departing with loved ones on the terrestrial plane was a sad experience, for many it was a joyful one as well to the extent we understood that life was cyclical and eternal in its energies.

This was originally our understanding of the meaning of "the resurrection and the life". Most ministers of the gospel of Black Liberation do not conduct funerals as such, but rather choose to relate to this rite as the celebration of a person's life. Black Folks in New Orleans have maintained an age old Afrikanism. After the interment of the deceased, they strike up the band and return home singing, dancing and rejoicing as they affirm the dearly departed has made it safely over the River into the realm of the Ancestors where they are now able to watch over and protect us.

UNITING THE MALE AND FEMALE PRINCIPLES IN THE SPIRIT OF ANGELS

In our closing comments, we think it fitting to touch on the coming together of the male/female principle through the dynamic cosmic expression of human sexuality. It cannot be over emphasized that this is a spiritual thing and it is with this understanding that you should come to one another. My brother, you must ever be mindful that the Black Female is the most sacred female entity in the world. Not only because of the joy derived from physical interchange with her, but also because of the spiritual enlightenment and growth which can be garnered from such encounters.

The ancient priests of Kemet were said to have attained phenomenal levels of spiritual growth and power through the practice of maithuna which was a total mental, physical and spiritual involvement with woman. Now there are European religious philosophers who believe that in order to achieve this spirituality you must be celibate. This is not the way for the Afrikan. So with that understanding, when you come together in the "midnight hour", assume the attitude of the sacredness of what you are doing. Try to ascertain the cosmic dynamics of what you are about to become involved in. While you are, as Aretha Franklin says, "getting in the spirit in the dark" strive to transcend the purely biological and become one in the One. In fact it is a good practice to include prayer; meditation and positive affirmations as a part of your love making. Be assured, if you are sincere in this, you will reach levels of joy and ecstasy that may exceed anything you have ever known before and then you will truly be communicating with angels.

The foregoing essays have presented just a few of the wondrous things the angelic essence of Afrikan Women stands for. So remember, as Haki Madhubuti says "Only fools limit their women".[93]

Preview

PREVIEW OF AFRIKAN GENESIS: *AN HISTORICAL REALITY*

In this collection of essays, we have touched on several dates, periods and ideas that perhaps we need to restate in chronological order.

About 200,000 years ago homo-sapiens (the first modern humans) emerged in southeast Alkebulan and nowhere else. The women of this group became the genetic mothers of all human beings who ever lived on the planet. Between 180,000-90,000 B.P., these Afrikans began migrating to other parts of the world carrying with them what some scientists refer to as "special advantages". Between 100,000-40,000 B.P., the Nubian progeny of this same racial stock journeyed to the European continent and settled there as they did in many other areas of the then known world.

Because recently a large cache of their fossil remains have been unearthed around Grimaldi, Italy, they have come to be known in some scientific circles as Nubian-Grimaldi. These Afrikans left to posterity some of the greatest art treasures the world has ever known. In fact, they were the first sophisticated artists; the first to duplicate the human form in accurate proportions. The most celebrated subject of their sculpture and other media was the Nubian-Grimaldi Woman, the original standard of grace and beauty on planet Earth.

So profound was the Nubian-Grimaldi male's reverence and adoration of her voluptuous charms, that figurine replicas of these Afrikan Women were buried with the deceased clutched affectionately to their chests as they lay in the fetal position. Some of these statuettes had arms in the shape of wings to signify the role of the Feminine Force in the transition of the human soul during the last rite of passage.

Either synonymous with or immediately following the Nubian-Grimaldi was a branch of Afrikan People known in the ancient world as Kushites—meaning people kissed of the sun—the archaic Kushites are difficult to chronicalize accurately because the period of their beginning is so remote in time, no one can say for sure when it started. We just know that they have been here for "a mighty long time".

These Black Folks who initially started out from the foot of the Mountains of the Moon by the Nile River created a civilization which covered the entire globe; among them the kingdoms, nations and empires of Kemet (Egypt), Phoenicia, Arabia, Chaldea, Persia and India just to mention a few. The kings, queens and nobility of the global Kushite Empire were the protagonists for all the legends, fables and mythologies of the ancient world.

One of the most sacred and guarded values in their societies was the honor and exaltation of the Feminine Principle as manifested in their women. Thus the power of the throne was vested in her and all lineage and property rights were the prerogative of her grace.

The immediate descendents of the Kushites—who encompassed a multiplicity of tribes and nations—were the Kemetans, misnomered Egyptians. The seminal stages of their empire began around 18,000 BCE—if legend be correct in reporting that Ausar and Auset, their first pharaoh and queen, were the founders of agriculture in that vicinity. Present scientific data puts the origin of agricultural science in the Nile Valley somewhere between 18,000-17,500 BCE.

One of the compelling features of Kemetan iconography and scenography is winged beings in attendance to and protecting the pharaoh, the most significant being that of Auset and Nephthys with arms that merge into wings. Among the many nations that borrowed from and adopted this type of symbology was Phoenicia, Sumer, Persia, Babylonia, Assyria and India. And at a much later date, the Hebrew-Israelites ca. 1240-200 BCE. All these initially Afrikan nations in turn modified and adapted the winged female emblems of Kemetan High Culture scientific symbology to serve their particular historical experiences and cultural needs at the time.

This is how the concept of guardian angels was born. It began with the Nubian-Grimaldi celebration of the manifold attributes of the Afrikan Woman; which was exalted to even higher levels of reverence by the Kushites who spread the concept all over the globe; stylized by the Kemetans in icons of Auset, Nephthys, Het-Heru and a host of other female deities; then grafted by the surrounding nations, including the Hebrews, into superhuman symbols of Divine communication and protection. The formulation of the idea of angels, which covers a time span from ca. 100,000 B.P. to the present, is predicated upon the once universal respect and reverence for Black Women that permeated the ancient world.

The awesome power of the Original Black Woman in the ancient world and the dynamic role she played in the creation stories of early humans is graphically sent forth and further explored in another work by this author entitled *Afrikan Genesis: Amazing Stories Of Man's Beginnings*. This book also presents some of the many remarkable ways our ancestors answered the eternal question, where did the world and human beings come from and recounts these historical narratives in terms of today's Black Experience. This work is destined to become one of the most widely read and talked about books in the Afrikan consciousness movement.

Afrikan Genesis takes you on a wonderful journey to distant lands and places in days of yore when Black People were building magnificent kingdoms and civilizations all around the globe. Among the many marvels of those golden ages were the creative learning systems and High Culture symbolic languages developed by ancient Afrikan scientists. Through the reading of this book, you can learn how to properly interpret the language of their mystic symbols and how to apply its powerful principles to improve the quality of your personal and professional life.

In those days there lived a people of great and wondrous intellect who composed amazing stories to explain the complex scientific principles of the origins of the world and of mankind. Many of these traditions have survived the ages and continue to enthral and capture the imagination of people all over the world today.

The Preface, entitled WHICH CAME FIRST, THE CHICKEN OR THE EGG, is a rational approach to the age old evolutionist versus creationist debate. Although many may claim to, no one knows for certain the actual process which brought about the creation of the world and human beings. Was it the evolutionary course of "natural selection" or the hand of a Cosmic Deity or perhaps both? Maybe man will never know, but the contemplation of these concept certainly do stimulate one's thought processes.

These are just two of the thirty provocative subjects covered in this work. *Afrikan Genesis: An Historical Reality* makes the scientific investigation of planet Earth's history and the evolution of man interesting and exciting to even the most casual reader.

The INTRODUCTION: AIN'T NOTHING LIKE THE REAL THING BABY deals with the cosmic purpose of the Black Race. Why the planet Earth was carefully prepared by billions and millions of years of change and formation to create the perfect environment for the emergence of the first human beings on Earth on the Mother Continent of Alkebulan.

These are just two of the seventeen provacative subjects covered in *Afrikan Genesis: Amazing Stories Of Man's Beginnings.* Here are some of the headings of the chapters from this series of studies;

Chapter One	Journey To The Ancient Afrikan Wisdom Of Astro-Mythological Cosmogony
Chapter Two	The Kemetan Cosmogonical Sphere In The Ancient World
Chapter Three	The Global Influence Of Ancient Afrikan Cosmogonical Science In Sumer and Arabia
Chapter Four	The Global Influence of Ancient Afrikan Cosmogonical Science In Old Persia
Chapter Five	Creation Science in India, Mystic Land Of The Black Buddhas
Chapter Six	Epic Poems Of Cosmic Heroes The Sacred Scriptures Of Cosmic Adventures
Chapter Seven	The Eternal Struggle Between Chaos and World Order: A Babylonian Creation Story
Chapter Eight	Anatomy Of A Cosmic Battle.

Afrikan Genesis: Amazing Stories of Man's Beginnings is Volume I of a four-volume series. In Volume II, *Afrikan Genesis: An Historical Reality,* we begin at 4.6 billion years ago, and take a spiritual fact finding journey through all the successive geological periods as we dock at each station along the way, we will carefully demonstrate their relevance to our people's historical reality.

Afrikan Genesis: An Historical Reality makes the scientific investigation of planet Earth's history and the evolution of man interesting and exciting to even the most casual reader.

Volume III, *Afrikan Genesis: A Narrative Commentary on the First Book of the Bible* is a verse by verse and story by story Afro-centric commentary on the Old Testament Book of Genesis which traces these scriptures back to the most ancient sacred writings of the *Book of the Coming Forth by Day and by Night* misnomered *The Egyptian Book of the Dead.*

Volume IV is entitled *Afrikan Genesis: Black Gods and Goddesses in the Land of Eden.* The basic objective of this work is to trace the gods and goddesses of worldwide mythologies, i.e., Kemetan, Greek, Roman, Scandinavian, etc., back to the original Afrikan kings and queens and heroes of whom they were symbols.

The above preview was presented as a cameo description of highlights from Volume I. We thought it appropriate to include this preview in the present collection of scholarly essays because the information we have already set forth in *Afrikan Woman: The Original Guardian Angel* is continually introduced and expanded upon in the *Afrikan Genesis* series. We trust that this brief introduction to the work will inspire and motivate our readers to acquire copies of same when it is published and investigate it further.

Until we meet again, may the peace, blessings, protection, and prosperity of our Afrikan Ancestors be with you and your loved ones for now and ever more and may the Creator grant us liberation in our lifetime. Amen

NOTES AND BIBLIOGRAPHY

1. *The Origin and Evolution of Religion,* Albert Churchward, George Allen and Unwin Ltd. London 1924. Reprinted by Health Research, P.O. Box 70, Mokelume Hill, Calif. 1986, p. 5.

2. *The Woman's Encyclopedia of Myths and Secrets,* Barbara G. Walker, Harper & Row, Publishers, San Francisco, Calif. 1983, p. 101.

3. *Ibid.* p. 35.

4. *The Description of Black Civilization,* Chancellor Williams, Third World Press, Chicago, Illinois, *Revised Edition*, 1974, Part I.

   Man, God, and Civilization, John G. Jackson, University Books, Inc., New Hyde Park, N.Y. 1972, p. 242.

5. *Black Male/Female Relationships,* Article The Neurological Misadventure of Primordial Man, by Edgar J. Ridley, Julia Hare - publisher, San Francisco, Calif. Autumn, 1982, pp. 56, 58.

6. *Authorized Version of the Holy Bible,* Daniel Chapter 7:9-10.

7. *Daily Life in Bible Times,* Albert Edward Bailey, Charles Scribner's Sons New York, N.W. 1943, p. 222.

8. *Man, God, and Civilization,* John G. Jackson, University Books, Inc., New Hyde Park, N.Y. 1972, p. 242.

9. *The Encyclopedia Brittannica,* Volume 1, 4th Edition. 1939, p. 920.

10. *World's Great Men of Color,* Volume I, J.A. Rogers, Helga M. Rogers, New York, N.Y. 1947, p. 116.

11. *Authorized Version of the Holy Bible*, Job Chapter 3:25; Proverbs Chapter 29:25.

12. *The Living Bible*, Tyndale House Publishers, Wheaton, Illinois. Coverdale House Publishers Ltd. London, England. Distributed by Doubleday and Company, Inc. Jeremiah Chapter 20:9.

13. *Harper's Bible Dictionary,* M.S. and J.L. Miler, Harper & Row Publishers, N.Y.C. 1961, p. 664.

14. *Ancient Egyptian Religion,* Henri Franfort, Harper & Row Publishers, N.Y.C. 1948, p. 6.

15. *Authorized Version of the Holy Bible*, 2 Samuel Chapter 22:1, 7, 11; Psalms 18: 7-9.

16. *Harper's Bible Dictionary*, (See above), p. 97.

17. *Authorized Version of the Holy Bible (KJV)*, Exodus 25:10, 11, 18-20, 22.

18. *Israel's Debt to Egypt*, Edward H. Sugden, The African Publication Society, (Dr. G.K. Osei) London, England. 1981. p. 84.

19. *Holy Bible (KJV)* Saint John 1:18.

20. *The Woman's Encyclopedia of Myths and Secrets*, Barbara G. Walker, (See above) p. 57.

21. *Ibid.*, p. 57

22. *Seventh-Day Adventist Bible Dictionary*, Siegfried H. Horn, Review and Herald Publishing Association, Washington, DC. 1960. p. 189.

23. *Stolen Legacy,* George G.M. James, Philosophical Library, N.Y.C. 1954. Reprinted by Julian Richardson Associates, San Francisco, Calif. 1976. pp. 40, 67, 131, 135.

24. *Harper's Bible Dictionary,* (See above), p. 98.

25. *The Woman's Encyclopedia of Myths and Secrets,* Barbara G. Walker (See above), p. 164.

Man, God, and Civilization, (See above) pp. 294, 137, 144.

26. *The Woman's Encyclopedia of Myths and Secrets,* Barbara G. Walker (See above) p. 355.

27. *Holy Bible (KJV),* Ezekiel 1:26-28

28. *The Great Mother,* Eric Neumann, Princeton University Press, 1963. pp. 98-99.

29. *The Woman's Encyclopedia of Myths and Secrets,* Barbara G. Walker (See above), p. 697.

30. *Black Woman In Antiquity,* Ivan Van Sertima/ Rosalind Jeffries, Thansaction Books, New Brunswick (U.S.A.) and London (U.K.) 1984, 1988. p. 120

31. *The Great Mother,* Eric Neuman, (See above), p. 328.

32. *The Woman's Encyclopedia of Myths and Secrets,* Barbara G. Walker, (See above), p. 267.

33. *Anacalypsis,* Volume I, Godfrey Higgins, London, 1836. Reprinted by Health Research, Mokelumne Hill, Calif. 1972. p. 518.

34. *Funk & Wagnall's New Encyclopedia,* Volume 18. 1983. p. 231.

35. *The Mysteries of Osiris' Ancient Egyptian Initiation,* R. Swinburne Clymer, The Philosophical Publishing Co., Quakertown, Penna. 1951. p. 128.

36. *The Great Mother,* Eric Neuman, (See above), p. 180.

The Signs and Symbols of Primordial Man, Albert Churchward, London & N.Y.C. 1913. Reprinted by Health Research, Mokelumne Hill, Calif. 1986. p. 160.

37. *The Woman's Encyclopedia of Myths and Secrets,* Barbara G. Walker, (See above), p. 270.

38. *Ibid.*, p. 271

39. *The Mysteries of Osiris' Ancient Egyptian Initiation,* R. Swinburne Clymer, (See above) p. 128

40. *Ibid.*, p. 157

41. *The Woman's Encyclopedia of Myths and Secrets,* Barbara G. Walker, (See above) p. 268.

42. *Ibid.*, p. 572.

43. *Ibid.*, p. 349.

44. *Afrikan People and European Holidays: A Mental Genocide,* Book Two, Ishakamusa barashango, IVth Dynasty Publishing Company, Washington, DC, February, 1983. p. 21.

45. *The Cultural Unity of Black Africa,* Cheikh Anta Diop, Third World Press, Chicago, Ill. 1978. pp. 127-128

46. *The Great Mother,* Eric Neuman (See above) pp. 275, 62.

47. *The Jesus Scroll,* Donovan Joyce, New American Library/ Times Mirror, 1972. pp. 76-77.

48. *Black Women In Antiquity,* Ivan Van Sertima/ Rosalind Jeffries, (See above), pp. 99,98.

49. *The Woman's Encyclopedia of Myths and Secrets,* Barbara G. Walker, (See above) p. 688.

50. *The Great Mother,* Eric Neuman (See above) p. 43.

51. *Afrikan People and European Holidays: A Mental Genocide,* Book Two, Ishakamusa Barashango, (See above), p. 22.

52. *The Cultural Unity of Black Africa,* Cheikh Anta Diop, (See above) p. 71.

53. *Wonderful Ethiopians of the Ancient Cushite Empire,* Drusilla Dunjee Houston, 1926. Republished by Black Classics Press, Baltimore, Md. 1985. p. 224.

54. *When God Was A Woman,* Merlin Stone, Harcourt Brace Jovanovich Publishing, San Diego, New York, London. 1976. pp. 2-3.

55. *The Woman's Encyclopedia of Myths and Secrets,* Barbara G. Walker, (See above), pp. 627,626.

56. *Black Women In Antiquity,* Ivan Van Sertima/John Henrik Clarke, (See above), p. 123.

57. *The Woman's Encyclopedia of Myths and Secrets,* Barbara G. Walker, (See above), p. 686.

58. *Man, God, and Civilization,* John G. Jackson, (See above), p. 22.

59. *Black Women In Antiquity,* Ivan Van Sertima/Rosalind Jeffries, (See above), p.99.

60. *African Presence In Early Europe,* Ivan Van Sertima/Legrand Clegg II, Transaction Books, New Brunswick (U.S.A.) and Oxford (U.K.) 1985. p. 28.

61. *The Great Mother,* Eric Neuman, (See above), p. 261.

62. *Ibid.,* p. 261.

63. *The World and Africa,* W.E. Burghardt DuBois, International Publishers, New York, 1946, 1965. pp. 87-88.

64. *Black Women in Antiquity,* Ivan Van Sertima/Rosalind Jeffries, (See above), p. 110.

65. *The Origin and Wvolution of Religion,* Albert Churchward, (See above), p. 198.

Isis Unveiled, Volume I, H.P. Blavatsky, Theosophical University Press, Pasadena, Calif. 1960. p. 147.

66. *The Woman's Encyclopedia of Myths and Secrets,* Barbara G. Walker, (See above), p. 695.

67. *Ibid.,* p. 697.

68. *The Holy Bible (KJV),* Saint Luke 3:22

69. *The Woman's Encyclopedia of Myths and Secrets,* Barbara G. Walker, (See above), p. 101.

70. *The Origin and Evolution of Religion,* Albert Churchward, (See above), p. 60.

71. *Black Women in Antiquity,* Ivan Van Sertima/Rosalind Jeffries, (See above), p. 116.

72. *The Jerusalem Bible,* Doubleday & Company, Inc., Garden City, New York, 1966. The Book of Wisdom 7:22-30; 8:1. pp. 1014-1015. Wisdom "She is a breath of the power God" Wisdom 7:22.

73. *The Holy Bible (KJV),* The Proverbs 8:1-3, 11, 12, 15, 16, 22.

The Living Bible, (See above), Proverbs 8:35.

74. *Black Women In Antiquity,* Ivan Van Sertima/Rosalind Jeffries, (See above), p. 104.

75. *The Great Mother,* Eric Neuman, (See above). p. 227.

76. *Ibid.*, p. 47.

77. *Ibid.*, pp. 42-43.

78. *Ibid.*, p. 128

79. *The Woman's Encyclopedia of Myths and Secrets,* Barbara G. Walker, (See above), p. 731.

80. *Stolen Legacy,* George G.M. James, (See above), p. 150.

81. *The Great Mother,* Eric Neuman, (See above), p. 326.

82. *Man, God, and Civilization,* John G. Jackson, (See above), p. 20.

83. *Blacks In Science: Ancient and Modern,* Ivan Van Sertima/Hunter Havelin Adams III, Transaction Books, New Brunswick (U.S.A.) and London (U.K.), 1983. pp. 27-28.

84. *The Great Mother,* Eric Newman, (See above), p. 226.

85. *The Origin and Evolution of Religion,* Albert Churchward, (See above) p. 246.

86. *The Woman's Encyclopedia of Myths and Secrets,* Barbara G. Walker, (See above), p. 68.

87. *The African Origin of Civilization: Myth or Reality,* Cheikh Anta Diop, Lawrence Hill & Company, New York and Westport, Paris 1955, New York 1974, p. 114

88. *Sex and Race,* Volume I, Joel A. Rogers, Helga M. Rogers, New York, N.Y., 1967. pp. 276, 281.

89. *Black Women In Antiquity,* Ivan Van Sertima/Rosalind Jeffries, (See above), pp. 120-121.

90. *African Origins of the Major "Western Religions",* Yosef ben Jochannan, Alkebulan Books, N.Y.C., 1970. pp. 199-201.

91. *The Interconnectedness of Life and Death: An African Perspective,* A Paper by Okomfo Kofi Boakye, Maat Institute for Human and Organizational Enhancement, Inc., Washington, DC (Bannaker City), April, 1987.

92. *The Iceman Inheritance: Prehistoric Sources of Western Man's Racism, Sexism and Aggression,* Michael Bradley, Warner Books, Inc., New York, N.Y. 10019, July, 1981.

93. *Rise Vision Comin,* Haki R. Madhubuti/Nation Liberation Art Ensemble, Nationhouse Positive Action Center, Washington, DC (Bannaker City), 1976.

ILLUSTRATIONS

Dedication — *Sex and Race,* Volume III, Joel A. Rogers, Helga M. Rogers, N.Y., N.Y. p.13

Plate 1 a. *Pharaohs of Egypt,* Horizon Magazine Editors, Jacquetta Hawkes author, American Heritage Publishing Company, Inc. p. 150. From the Egyptian Museum, Cairo.

b. *Egyptian Mythology,* Veronica Ions, Paul Hamlyn, The Hamlyn Publishing Group Ltd. London, New York, Sydney, Toronto. p. 64.

c. *Tutankhamon,* Edward L. Jones, Seattle, Washington p. 92. From the Metropolitan Museum of Art.

Plate 2 — *Pharaohs of Egypt,* (See above). p. 101. From the British Museum.

Plate 3 a. *Osiris and the Egyptian Resurrection,* Volume I. E.A. Wallis Budge, Dover Publications, Inc., New York. p. 20.

b. *Tutankhamon,* (See above). From Metropolitan Museum of Art, photographed by Harry Burton. p. 76.

c. *Ancient Egypt: Three Thousand Years of Splendor,* Warner A. Hutchinson, Grosset & Dunlap. A Filmways Company, New York. p. 86.

Plate 4 — *Osiris and the Egyptian Resurrection,* Volume I. (See above). p. 29.

Plate 5 a. *Osiris and the Egyptian Resurrection,* Volume II. (See above). p. 31. From Mariette, *Denderah,* IV, 70.

b. *Ancient Egypt,* Lionel Casson and the Editors of Time-Life Books, Time Incorporated, New York pp. 184, 185.

Plate 6 a. *When God Was A Woman,* Merlin Stone, Harcourt Brace Jovanovich, Publishers. San Diego, New York, London. Illustration 11. From Museum of Fine Arts, Boston.

b. *Tutankhamon,* (See above). p. 96. From Metropolitan Museum of Art, photographed by Harry Burton.

c. *Ibid.,* (See above). p. 97. (See above)

Plate 7 *The Great Mother,* Erich Neumann, Princeton University Press. Plate 4.

Plate 8 a. *Egyptian Mythology,* (See above). p. 137.

b. *The Great Mother,* (See above). Plate 91.

Plate 9 *Bible Places: Historical Geographic Highlights,* Antoinette Mitchell, designed by Tyyne Hakola, The C.R. Gibson Company, Norwalk, Connecticut. p. 39.

Plate 10 *Metu Teggkhet,* artist, Ausar-Auset Society, Brooklyn, New York.

Plate 11a. *Osiris and the Egyptian Resurrection,* Volume II, (See above). p. 22. (See above).

b. *Osiris and the Egyptian Resurrection,* Volume I, (See above). p. 249. From Mariette, *Abydos,* Volume I, Plate 17.

Plate 12a. *The Culture of Ancient Egypt,* John A. Wilson, The University of Chicago Press, Chicago and London. Figure 31c.

b. *The Great Mother,* (See above). Plate 157B.

c. *Ibid.,* (See above). Plate 130.

d. *Ibid.,* (See above). Plate 126.

Plate 13 *Abingdon Bible Handbook,* Edward P. Blair, Abingdon Press, Nashville and New York. p. 64. From The Oriental Institute, The University of Chicago.

Plate 14a. *Newsweek,* January 11, 1988, 444 Madison Avenue, N.Y.C. 10022. p. 50 Artist I. B. Ohlsson.

b. *The African Origin of Civilization: Myth or Reality,* Cheikh Anta Diop, Lawrence Hill & Co., New York and Westport. p. 270.

c. *The Great Mother,* (See above). Plate 1.

Plate 15a. *The Great Mother,* (See above). p. 327 Figure 73. From the Roda Bible, XI Century.

b. *The Origin and Evolution of Religion,* Albert Churchward, George Allen & Unwin Ltd., London. p. 240. Drawn by K. Watkins.

Plate 16 *Metu Teggkhet,* artist, (See above)

a. The *ba* bird, a Kemetan symbol of the human soul comparable to the Kushite-Hindu *shakti*. Note female features of the head.

Falcon protective divinity symbol hovers above head of Rameses II.

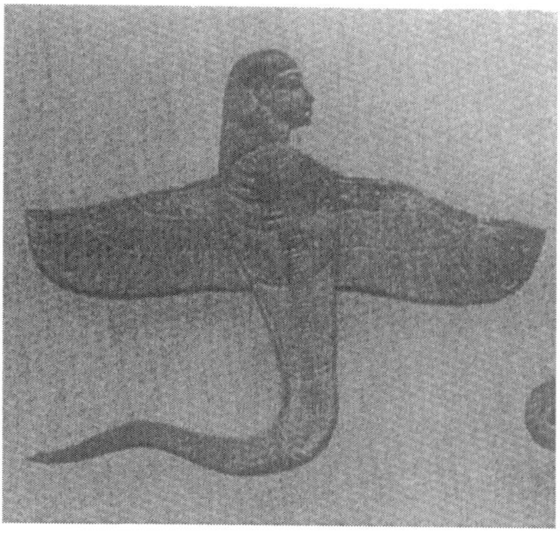

c. Flying serpent with human head. A Kemetan symbol for elevated intellect and spiritual ascendency. Models of this type inspired Sumerian, Babylonian, Assyrian and Hebrew seraphim imagery.

A Kemetan judgement scene. Ausar strengthened by Auset and Nebthet.

Plate 2

a. European artist's conception of an original Afrikan iconograph from the Papyrus of Hunefer.

b. Auset (Isis) with throne headdress.

c. Nebethet (Nephthys) with incense burner headdress.

Plate 3

A European corruption of a bas-relief at Philae, Egypt depicting Ausar safe and secure in the wings of Black Angels, Auset and Nephthys.

Plate 4

a. Ausar (Osiris) being re-energized for resurrection by Auset, Nephthys and Het-Heru represented as hawks.

b. Outline drawings of Auset the power and protector of the throne. Nephthys the spiritual essence and transcendent wisdom of the pharaoh. Het-Heru (Hathor) goddess of love, happiness and beauty.

a. Icon of the winged Auset wearing the throne headdress. Rediscovered in a pyramid in modern day Kush (Ethiopia).

b. Throne decorated with the wings of Auset.

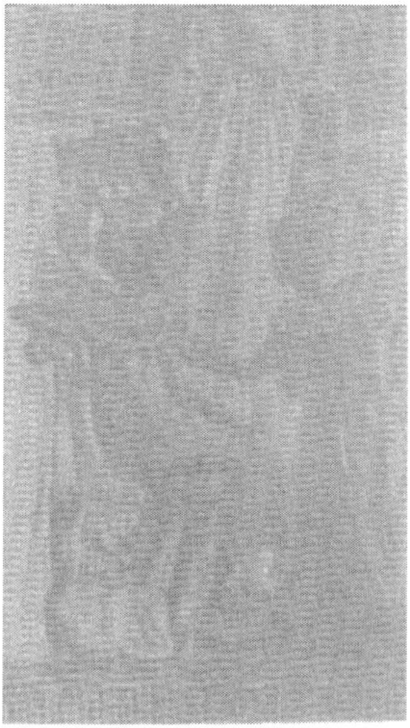

c. Pharaoh Tutankhamon being annointed for kingship by the queen who represents his sour of stately power.

Plate 6

of the throne. In this engraving she wears the headdress of Het-Heru to emphasize her maternal aspects.

Plate 7

a. Nut-the sky goddess, carved inside of the lid of a coffin denoting the spirit of the Feminine Energy Force, would comfort the deceased through all eternity.

b. Nut engraved in interior of coffin bottom.

Plate 8

Artist conception of the Ark of the Covenant. Re-Afrikanized by this author.

An historically correct portrayal of **Ausar**, **Auset**, and **Nebthet**.

Plate 10

a. Auset and Nephthys protecting and preparing the body of Ausar for resurrection. Shown here without their wings.

b. Nebthet (Nephthys), Het-Heru and Auset protecting the pharaoh and infusing him with their genius powers.

a. An ivory Phoenician sphinx with wings rediscovered in Palestine.

b. Khart Haddas (Carthagian) stone monument engraved with an angel image.

c. Aryanized version of an original Kushite-India goddess. Probably a symbol of the *shakti* spirit which was said to guide and comfort a man through life and death.

d. Lilith, a *shakti* symbol of ancient Sumer signifying the spirit which embraced the deceased and carried them to the nether world.

Plate 12

Winged bull cherub guarding the throne room of Sargon II, King of Babylon. A transmogrification of Kemetan female guardian angels.

Genetic Clues

Our cells carry the history of mankind's development, a path scientists followed toward Eve.

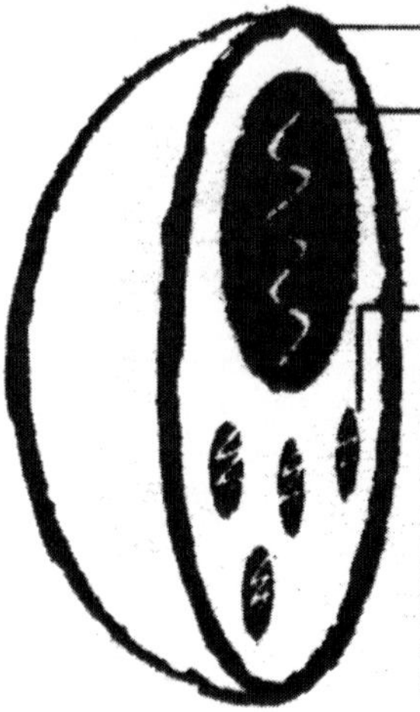

a. Artist conception of the mitochondrial DNA in the human cell.

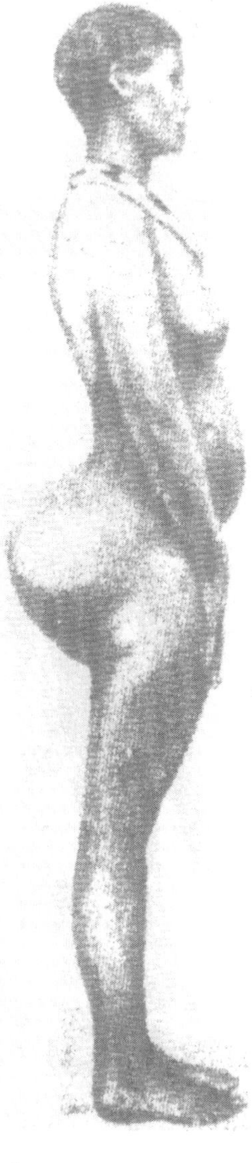

b. The original "Sapphire Ev probably favored this depi of a Koisan woman of the Kalahari.

c. Type of figurine unearthed in Nubian-Grimaldi graves in many geographical locations. This was found in Austria and misnomered Venus of Willendorf.

Plate 14

Plate 15

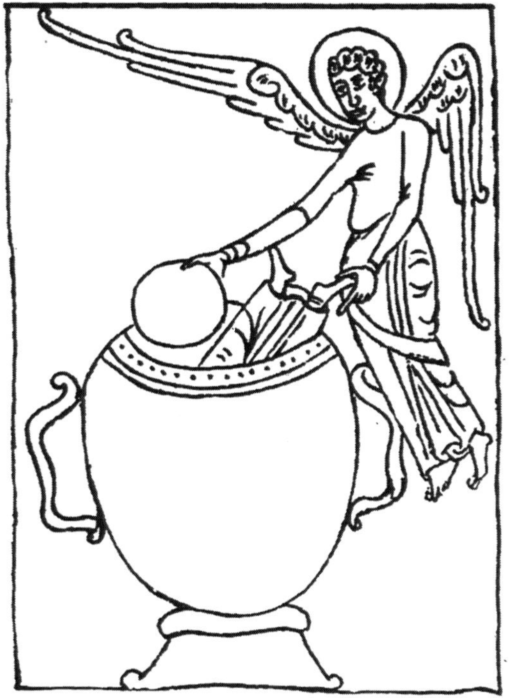

a. Artist sketch from the 11th Century of a baptismal urn in the shape of an egg used in Euro-Christian rebirth rituals.

b. Lightened version of a very pigmented image of Ptah fashioning the cosmic egg of the world upon a potter's wheel. Signifying the male role in procreation.

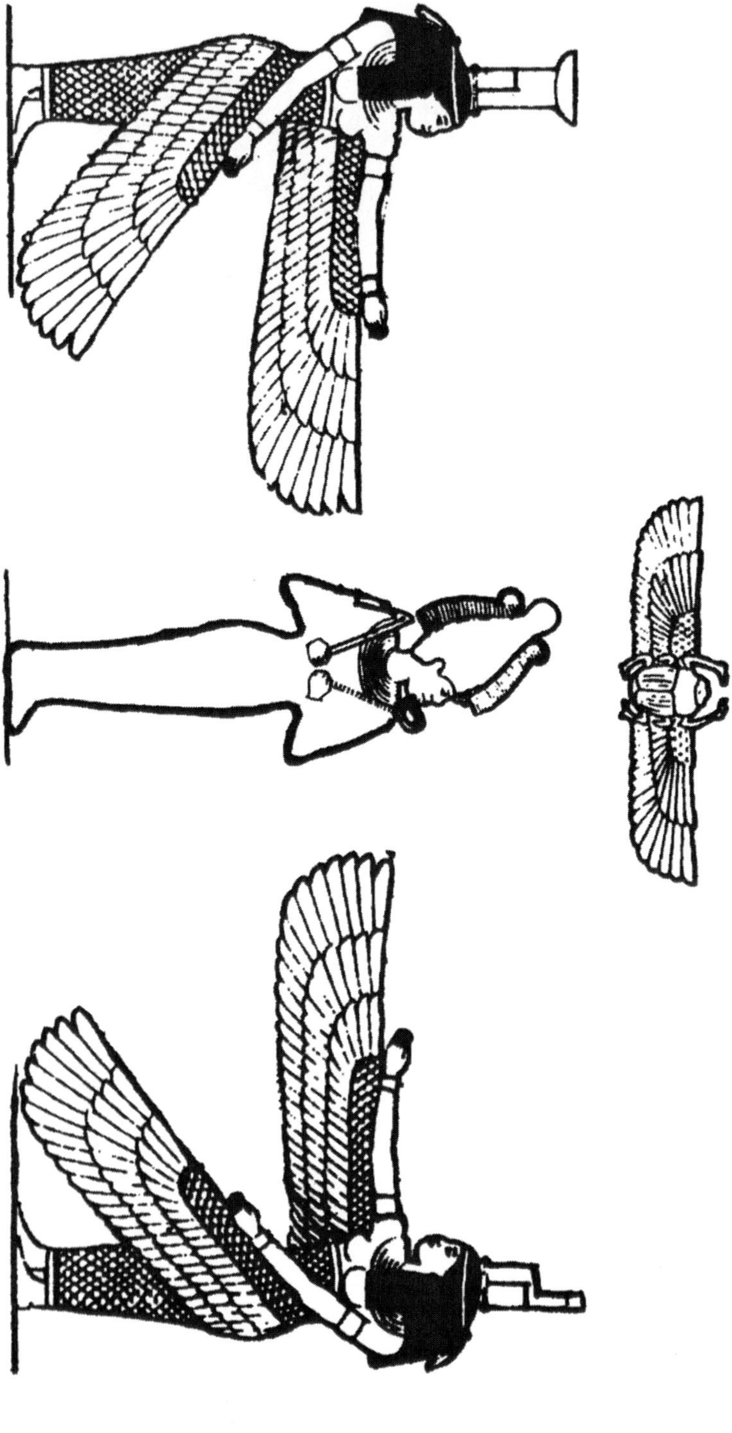

ANGEL HEART POSTERS

Prints, pencil autographed by the artist, of *Angel Heart* are available in two sizes; 22x28 and 14x17.

ORDER FORM

☐ Angel Heart, 22x28 inches, *Postpaid* $20.00 Units ___

☐ Angel Heart, 14x17 inches, *Postpaid* $15.00 Units ___

NAME ______________________________

ADDRESS ______________________________

CITY/STATE ______________________________ ZIP ________

Total Amount Enclosed ________

Remit to: Mr. Cal Massey
509 Dawson Street
Moorestown, NJ 08057

Make check or money order payable to Cal Massey.

- Please allow 2 weeks for delivery -

AUDIO CASSETTE TAPE LIBRARY

FEATURING THE WORKS OF

Dr. Ishakamusa Barashango

1.

THE REAL JESUS WAS A BLACK MAN

This cassette is a very special version of the subject, "Will The Real Jesus Please Stand Up?" delivered at the Slave Theater in Brooklyn, N.Y., May 31, 1992. Throughout the course of this lecture, Barashango presents the listener with an array of rediscovered historical data on the Afrikan origin of and the initial intent of the early Christian movement. No matter what your belief system, you will find this message to be engaging and mentally stimulating. Full 90 min. tape $10.00.

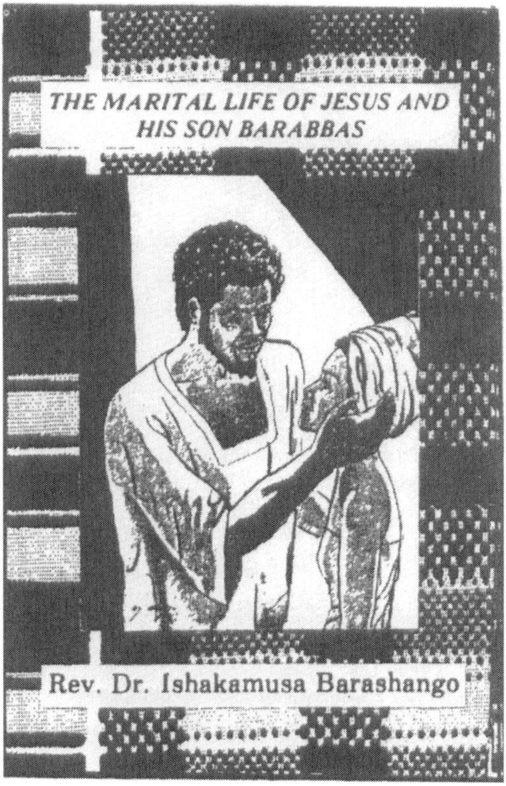

2.

THE MARITAL LIFE OF JESUS AND HIS SON BARABBAS

This message clearly and logically sets forth the historical realities of the life and times of Jesus Christ, the Black Messiah. With emphasis on his apparent marriage as alluded to in the Bible and indicated in the Hebrew Laws and customs of that time. The role of his eldest son in the struggle for the liberation of Judea from the white Roman power structure is also explained along with surprising facts concerning Jesus' family life. This cassette is well documented with biblical and historical data, presented in an interesting style. Full 90 min. tape $10.00

3.

BLACK HISTORICAL FACTS ON THE LIFE OF JESUS, VOLUME I

Most of us living today have been somewhat familiarized with the teachings of Jesus through the theological perspective espoused by the nominal Christian Churches, yet so few are cognizant of the life and times of the real Jesus as verified by a scientific investigation of documented historical fact. In this presentation, Black Liberation Theologian Rev. Dr. Ishakamusa Barashango shares with you that which he has been privileged to draw from the vast reservoir of knowledge garnered and preserved by some of the greatest Black minds of our times. Full 90 min. tape $10.00

4.

BLACK HISTORICAL FACTS ON THE LIFE OF JESUS, VOLUME II

Volume II is a continuation of the historical information set forth in volume I, and like it, is based on well documented evidence and analytical inquiry delivered in the language of every day people and the dynamic style for which Bro. Barashango is so very well known. This offering broaches such relevant points as to how the foundations of Eurocentric Christianity were laid by the military power of the Roman Empire and how the original teaching of Jesus Christ was co-opted and recast in the image of white supremacist dogma as they wrestled control of Christendom from the original Afrikan Church. Full 90 min. tape $10.00

AMAZING BLACK FACTS OF THE BIBLE: AN HISTORICAL OUTLINE

Rev. Dr. Ishakamusa Barashango

5.

AMAZING BLACK FACTS OF THE BIBLE: AN HISTORICAL OUTLINE

Truly this cassette will make your Bible come brilliantly alive with the beauty of it's Afrikan historicity beginning with the ancient depiction's of Almighty God and the vivid descriptions of Adam and Eve through synoptic sketches of Noah's ark and the flood story. This tape also includes a factual discussion of the migrations of the children of Ham - which despel the myth of the curse of Ham, Nimrod and the East Ethiopian Empire, The story of Abraham, Isaac, and Jacob, Moses and his Egyptian high culture education and the genetic ties of Israel with Egypt and Ethiopia. Full 90 min. tape $10.00

6.

AFRIKAN ORIGIN OF THE CHRISTIAN CHURCH

This tape abounds in clearly understandable historical data. In this presentation Barashango refers all the way back to the Palestine of circa 50,000 - 70,000 years ago, and through scientific evidence verifies the presence of it's original Black inhabitants. Through historical narrative he traces the settlement of the Africoid Hebrews in the land of Canaan, then goes on to delineate the historical events which led up to the life and times of Jesus the Black Messiah, the rise and establishment of the original African Church in that region and it's eventual co-optation and corruption by the Roman Empire. Full 90 min. tape $10.00

7.

BLACK WOMAN: QUEEN MOTHER OF THE UNIVERSE

This cassette is a special and uniquely different rendition of excerpts from the book, *Afrikan Woman: The Original Guardian Angel,* delivered at the Shrine of the Black Madonna in Houston, Texas. "Overwhelming archaeological, anthropological, and historical documentation has revealed beyond a shadow of a doubt that the Afrikan Woman was the first beauty queen on Earth and as such she was projected into the heavens and enshrined in the hearts of the people of the early civilizations as the Queen Of Heaven, The Mother Goddess, The Creatress of All Living Things." Full 90 min. tape $10.00

8.

AFRIKAN ORIGIN OF THE HUMAN SPECIES

It was in keeping with historical reality that this enlightening yet oftimes rather humorous lecture was delivered at Morgan State University, Baltimore, Maryland. It enthusiastically covers a time line beginning with the evolution of the first humans on the Mother Continent around 15 million years before the present and their subsequent migrations from the foot of the Mountains of the Moon in the heartland of Afrika, then traces their settlement over the entire planet from the early stages until the establishment of the global High Culture Civilizations of the Ancient Kushite Empire. Full 90 min. tape $10.00

9.

IN THE BEGINNING WAS THE BLACK RACE

Starting with Genesis 1:26-28 "Let us make Man in our image after our likeness...." and selected readings from his book, *Afrikan Genesis: Amazing Stories Of Man's Beginnings*, Dr. Barashango presents an Afrikan Centered interpretation of this text based on the hard evidences of historical reality. During this dissertation he also explores certain aspects of this subject which may not have been previously considered, then sets forth these age old traditions relative to today's scientific rediscoveries. Full 90 min. tape $10.00

10.

PORTRAIT OF THE ETERNAL PEOPLE

The historical collage depicted in this album is drawn from the palette of the indisputable evidences of documented fact, stroked by the brush of sincerity and undying love. This offering helps to restore the true "knowledge of self" which once was lost to us through a descriptive overview of marvelous periods of Black Civilization from the creation of planet Earth to the glory of the Blackamoors in Spain and the Afrikan rediscovery of "America" almost two centuries before the voyages of Columbus. Full 90 min. ape $10.00

11.

AND THE WORD OF THE LORD CAME BY MARCUS GARVEY

This cassette is a very good introduction to the life and teachings of the Honorable Marcus Mosiah Garvey, who on one occasion in his eventful life asked the question "Where is the Black Man's Government, where is his king and his kingdom, where is his president, his country, and his ambassador, his army, his men of big affairs? I could not find them and then I declared, I will help to make them. Surely every Black man, woman, and child should know about this superb and noble Afrikan. Full 90 min tape $10.00

12.

THE GOSPEL ACCORDING TO OL'NAT THE PROPHET

On October 1, 1983, the eve of the 183rd anniversary of Nat Turner's birth, a collective of community based businesses and organizations came together at AFCOM Learning Center in Richard Allen City(Philadelphia, Pa.) to pay tribute to the spirit of this extraordinary New Afrikan patriot. During his presentation Bro. Barashango explores the life's work and teachings of Nat Turner and other preachers of righteousness who propagated the gospel of Black Liberation. Full 90 min. tape $10.00

13. .

A BLACK REVOLUTIONARY CALLED JESUS

At the onset of his ministry, Jesus of Nazareth procalimed to the Hebrews in Galilee "The spirit of the Lord is upon me; he has appointed me to preach good news to the poor; he has sent me to heal the broken hearted and to announce that captives shall be freed from their oppressors, and that God is ready to give blessings to all who come to him." Luke 4:18-19 (The Living Bible Translation). Historically, what was this strong and militant statement taken to mean and if, as many have claimed, Jesus was a non-violent pacifist, why did he instruct his disciples, "....he that hath a purse, let him take it, and likewise his scrip: and he that hath no sword, let him sell his garment and buy one." Luke 22:36. These and other important historical points of intrest are discussed in this message which is a sequel to the audio cassette "The Real Jesus Was A Black Man." Full 90 min. tape $10.00

14.

AFRIKAN WARRIORS IN THE BIBLE

Some have observed that it seems as though the only people in this world who let their religious beliefs get in the way of defending themselves is the "Negro Christian". Actually most of the stories in the Bible do not teach non violent pacifism. For example the scriptures report that "the man Moses was very meek, above all the men which were upon the face of the earth " Numbers 12:3, yet it is also written Moses slew Sihon King of the Amorites and Og, King of Bashan with the sword, Deuteronomy 1:4. At another time Jesus of Nazareth declared "Think not that I am come to send peace on Earth: I came not to send peace, but a sword." Matthew 10:34. Revelations 19:11 describes his return to earth thusly, "And I saw heaven opened, and behold a white horse and he that sat upon him...in righteousness he doth make war. In this message Dr. Barashango examines the dynamic exploits of a long list of Biblical warriors. Full 90 min. tape $10.00

15.

HOW TO FIND BLACK HISTORY IN THE BIBLE

Although many may not be aware of it, in it's original form the Bible was an Afrikan history book composed by the Afrikan Israelites based on the chronicles, oral traditions and religious philosophy of a small Black Judean nation in Palestine. Today the Bible in it's present form has been co-opted, corrupted and twisted into a tool for the manipulation of the masses of the people especially Afrikans and other peoples of color by foriegn invaders of this ancient Black land. Therefore one of the sacred missions of Afrikan Centered Scholars in these times is to reclaim that which was ours in the first place and reinstate the Bible as an instrument of liberation by historically taking it back to it's Afrikan roots. That is the main objective of this message presented by Brother Barashango on one of his many lecture tours through the Southern U.S.. Full 90 min. tape $10.00

16.

RESURRECTING THE HIDDEN COSMIC POWERS OF THE AFRIKAN MIND

Our awesome mental powers are often hidden from us because many times our knowledge of self is cloaked in someone else's image. Thus this message earnestly seeks to help us heal this pathological state through a discourse on the effective use of your most precious personal possession---your mind. Instructions are given as to how to tap the eternal energies of your inner self. This lecture reveals the master key to personal power and outlines a seven-step formula for achieving your objectives and enhancing the quality of your life. It also explores some of the ancient secrets of obtaining and maintaining peace of mind and cosmic consciousness. This cassette really puts you in touch with your true self. Full 90 min. tape $10.00

❊ MAIL ORDER FORM ❊

When ordering audio tapes list how many of each selection You desire in the corresponding numbered box.

1. *The Real Jesus Was A Black Man* ——————————
2. *The Marital Life Of Jesus And His Son Barabbas* ——————
3. *Black Historical Facts On The LIfe Of Jesus Volume I* ——————————
4. *Black Historical Facts On The Life Of Jesus Volume II* ——————————
5. *Amazing Black Facts Of The Bible: An Historical Outline* ——————————
6. *Afrikan Origin Of The Christian Church* ——————
7. *Black Woman Queen Mother Of The Universe* ——————
8. *Afrikan Origin Of The Human Species* ——————
9. *In The Beginning Was The Black Race* ——————
10. *Portrait Of The Eternal People* ——————————
11. *The Gospel According To Ol' Nat The Prophet* ——————
12. *And The Word Of The Lord Came By Marcus Garvey* ————
13. *A Black Revolutionary Called Jesus* ——————————
14. *Afrikan Warriors In The Bible* ——————————
15. *How To Find Black History In The Bible* ——————
16. *Resurrecting The Hidden Cosmic Powers Of The Afrikn Mind* ——————————
17. *The Bible: Word Of God Or Work Of Man* ——————
18. *It's Madness! Black People And Whitefolks Holidays: Dr. Barashango In Concert From A Hip Hop Perspective* ————
19. *Great Black Women In The Bible Pt. 1* ——————————
20. *Great Black Women Of The Bible Pt. 2* ——————————
21. *The Historical Reality: Christopher Columbus DID NOT Discover America* ——————————
22. *Afrikan People And European Holidays:A Mental Genocide, The Tape (Misgivivg Day)* ——————
23. *Afrikan People And European Holidays:A Mental Genocide, The Tape (Xmas)* ——————————
24. *Kwanzaa In The Bible* ——————————

PLEASE TURN PAGE FOR MAILING INSTRUCTIONS

❊ MAIL ORDER FORM ❊

When ordering audio tapes list how many of each selection You desire in the corresponding numbered box.

1. *The Real Jesus Was A Black Man* ——————————
2. *The Marital Life Of Jesus And His Son Barabbas* ——————
3. *Black Historical Facts On The LIfe Of Jesus Volume I* ——————————
4. *Black Historical Facts On The Life Of Jesus Volume II* ——————————
5. *Amazing Black Facts Of The Bible: An Historical Outline* ——————————
6. *Afrikan Origin Of The Christian Church* ——————————
7. *Black Woman Queen Mother Of The Universe* ——————————
8. *Afrikan Origin Of The Human Species* ——————————
9. *In The Beginning Was The Black Race* ——————————
10. *Portrait Of The Eternal People* ——————————
11. *The Gospel According To Ol' Nat The Prophet* ——————————
12. *And The Word Of The Lord Came By Marcus Garvey* ——————
13. *A Black Revolutionary Called Jesus* ——————————
14. *Afrikan Warriors In The Bible* ——————————
15. *How To Find Black History In The Bible* ——————————
16. *Resurrecting The Hidden Cosmic Powers Of The Afrikn Mind* ——————————
17. *The Bible: Word Of God Or Work Of Man* ——————————
18. *It's Madness! Black People And Whitefolks Holidays: Dr. Barashango In Concert From A Hip Hop Perspective* ——————
19. *Great Black Women In The Bible Pt. 1* ——————————
20. *Great Black Women Of The Bible Pt. 2* ——————————
21. *The Historical Reality: Christopher Columbus DID NOT Discover America* ——————————
22. *Afrikan People And European Holidays:A Mental Genocide, The Tape (Misgivivg Day)* ——————————
23. *Afrikan People And European Holidays:A Mental Genocide, The Tape (Xmas)* ——————————
24. *Kwanzaa In The Bible* ——————————

PLEASE TURN PAGE FOR MAILING INSTRUCTIONS

210818-300-3-60W